A Law Enforcement Officer's Guide to Testifying in DWI and Other Cases

A Law Enforcement Officer's Guide to Testifying in DWI and Other Cases

James M. Vukelic

Carolina Academic Press
Durham, North Carolina

Library of Congress Cataloging-in-Publication Data

Vukelic, James M., 1950- author.
A law enforcement officer's guide to testifying in DWI and other cases / James M. Vukelic.
pages cm
Includes bibliographical references and index.
ISBN 978-1-61163-750-2 (alk. paper)
1. Police witnesses--United States. 2. Drunk driving--Investigation--United States. 3. Police--United States--Handbooks, manuals, etc. I. Title.

KF9673.5.V85 2015
345.73'0247--dc23

2015004580

Carolina Academic Press
700 Kent Street
Durham, NC 27701
Telephone (919) 489-7486
Fax (919) 493-5668
www.cap-press.com

Printed in the United States of America

To my son-in-law, Shaun, and all of the other law enforcement officers who so competently serve and protect us; and to my son, Reed, and all of the others in our military who do the same in the air, on land, and sea. I salute you.

Contents

Foreword

The overall purpose for writing this book is to reduce the carnage on our highways caused by impaired driving. If officers make good arrests and can effectively articulate why they did so, more convictions should result and our impaired driving laws will serve as a better deterrent. A secondary goal is to reduce the stress attendant to testifying in court. As one neurologist noted, we become less anxious and better able to recall details when our stress level is low. One of the best ways to reduce stress is to prepare for the anxiety-producing event; for officers, that event is the trial. This book should assist officers in that preparation and thereby make them more comfortable on the witness stand.

As a former judge, administrative hearing officer, and prosecutor, I have heard thousands of DWI cases. From those cases, I have a good sense of the questions defense attorneys typically ask in DWI cases and have included many of them in this book. Sometimes a suggested response or warning is offered. The suggested responses are not necessarily better than those an officer might give without reference to this book but knowing the questions in advance gives an officer time to construct a truthful answer. Forewarned is forearmed.

Another advantage to becoming familiar with questions often posed by defense attorneys is that it may help an officer modify and improve standard operating procedures. While defense attorneys can be creative and come up with new angles to discredit an officer's testimony, many of the tactics described in this book have been used for decades. It is doubtful those tactics will be abandoned anytime soon because they are often successful. For example, if officers know that defense attorneys will likely ask questions about weather conditions at the time of the stop because those conditions can impact field sobriety testing, officers may be persuaded to include those details in their incident reports.

Our justice system is built on the theory that when two opponents are evenly matched, each will bring out the strengths of his own case and the weaknesses of the opposition. In theory, the truth emerges from this adversary process and justice is served. This book will help officers become better at their craft and make them stronger allies in the search for truth.

A Law Enforcement Officer's Guide to Testifying in DWI and Other Cases

Chapter One

What You Need to Understand before Trial

Section One: Trials Are Civilized Battles

> "A trial is still an ordeal by battle. For the broadsword there is the weight of evidence; for the battle-ax the force of logic; for the sharp spear, the blazing gleam of truth; for the rapier, the quick and flashing knife of wit."—Lloyd Paul Stryker

Modern disputes are played out every day in thousands of courts across our land. But it was not always this way. Our legal roots go back to England where, centuries ago, most disputes were handled by the church courts. In medieval times, people assumed God would sort out the guilty from the innocent. Punishment was designed to deter others from sinning but leave the sinner alive and able to repent. This was often accomplished by severing the hands, feet, or genitals of the sinner.

In those days, populations were sparse and few people traveled. Like life in many small towns today, everyone knew their neighbors. Consequently, it was not difficult to figure out who the culprit was in most cases. Sometimes, though, guilt was not clear. In those cases the Church used the "ordeal" to settle matters. The most common methods of the ordeal were by hot iron, cold water, cursed morsel, and battle.

In the ordeal by hot iron, the accused was made to hold a red-hot iron for a brief time. His hand was wrapped in cloth and inspected three days later. If it was healing, that was evidence from God that he was innocent. If it had begun to fester, he was guilty.

In the ordeal by cold water, the accused was bound and lowered into a pool on a rope. If he sank, he was innocent and was pulled out, still alive, and set free. If he floated, he was guilty and treated accordingly.

In the ordeal of the cursed morsel, the accused was forced to swallow a piece of dry bread with a feather in it. If he did not choke on the bread, he was proved innocent.

The ordeal by battle was used when two people accused each other of crimes or when they disagreed over the ownership of property. The two fought to the death. If a woman challenged a man, he was buried waist-deep in the ground as a handicap. Lords could avoid injury or death by hiring someone to fight for them, a "champion," as they came to be called. Two champions might have a sword fight or joust on horseback to determine the outcome of the dispute. The duel, recognized by courts as a permissible means of solving disputes in the United States as late as 1819, was a successor to the ordeal by battle.

In the thirteenth century, the ordeal was replaced with the forerunner of our modern jury. In what was called a "wager of law," someone accused of a crime could bring an "oathhelper" to swear that the defendant was a truthful man. He might then be exonerated. Over the years that followed, a presenting jury comprising as many as forty-eight men determined guilt, not on the basis of testimony or evidence, but on the basis of their own knowledge or what they could find out.

A defendant who objected to a jury trial could be imprisoned or tortured by being made to lie on the ground, his chest loaded with successively heavier weights until he either submitted to trial by jury or died. Many were willing to die rather than submit to jury trial because the real estate of a convicted felon went to the king for a year and a day, and then went to his lord permanently, thus impoverishing his family.

Beginning around 1450, jurors no longer spoke of their own knowledge but heard witnesses. By the sixteenth century, the jury operated in roughly the same way it does today. While there are many who criticize the jury system, it has developed into a means by which citizens protect themselves from an oppressive government, characterized by overly strict legislation or prosecution.

The jury has come full circle, from a group of neighbors who knew best the facts underlying a dispute, to a group of "peers" who have no personal knowledge of the case. We have parted from the manner in which our European ancestors conducted trials.

In several European countries today, judges take nearly complete control of litigation. The judge selects the witnesses, questions them, and decides the case.

In our country, the impartiality of the decision-maker is preserved by the noninvolvement of the judge until trial begins. While lawyers may toil with a case for months and even years before trial, the judge often becomes acquainted with the facts and issues for the first time at trial. This reduces the bias inherent in the decision-making process.

Still, the trial is a battle. Opponents no longer fight to the death, but modern dispute resolution in court is nevertheless a form of warfare. Only now we are more civilized. Instead of using lances or swords, we fight in court with witnesses and exhibits. The modern witness must remember, though, it is still a battle. Instead of champions, lawyers joust with words and pictures as their weapons of choice.

In every battle, civilized or not, there are two opponents, diametrically opposed to one another. Our laws are premised on the belief that two evenly matched adversaries will bring out the strengths of their own cause and the weaknesses of the other. It is hoped this adversary system will illuminate the truth for the finder-of-fact, whether that be a judge or jury.

A witness will always be seen by one party as a friend; the opposing party will take a contrary view. Regardless of how professional you appear, how unbiased and impartial your view of the case, you will be treated by one side as a comrade and as an adversary by the other.

The simple truth is your testimony helps one side and hurts the other. If this were not so, you would not be called to testify in the first place. If you do not fully appreciate the battleground for what it is, you may be surprised, affronted, or both when you take the witness stand. To be forewarned is to be forearmed.

Section Two: Flight or Fight

In most cases, you will have a natural tendency to support one side or the other in the litigation. If you are a law enforcement officer, you will almost always identify with the prosecution and hope for a conviction.

When you testify, your credibility is at stake. Indeed, it is one of the favorite targets for opposing counsel. This usually takes the form of attacks based on your perception, knowledge of the facts, any bias or prejudice you may have, or your recollection of the events about which you are called upon to testify. These modes of attack, or impeachment as it is called in court, will be discussed later at greater length.

Courtrooms are stress-inducing arenas. Psychologists have long identified the human reaction to stressful situations by describing the "flight or fight response." When faced with acute stress our heart beats faster, our digestive system shuts down or slows down so more blood flows to our arms and legs, and our adrenalin level increases. We gear up to fight or skedaddle just as our ancestors did when faced with saber-toothed tigers and other menaces.

When on the witness stand, even trial veterans, people who have testified many times in the past, will tell you they often experience anxiety. Part of that is created by the atmosphere: a room devoid of personality and warmth, a stern-looking judge in a black robe peering down at you from on high, and an opposing attorney poised to rip your heart out in pursuit of a client's cause. While these are not the reality in every courtroom, they can and do create a hostile environment.

Unfortunately, there is no opportunity for "flight." Witnesses usually come to court under subpoena, meaning they must attend or be found in contempt of court. The alternative is to "fight." No physical altercation is anticipated but a battle of wits may ensue between the witness and opposing counsel.

Like it or not, you will probably become emotionally invested in the process, if not the outcome of the trial. You will want to "win." At a minimum, you will want your testimony to be accepted as factual and truthful, even if it does not determine the verdict. You will want to be viewed as a credible person.

The objective of this book is to increase the odds that your testimony will be well-received by the judge or jury. To accomplish that objective, you must be able to help the judge or jury understand and accept your point of view.

Section Three: How the Legal Process Works

There are two kinds of cases: criminal and civil. In criminal cases, the accused is brought to court in answer to charges filed by the prosecutor. The prosecutor represents a governmental body: federal, state, or local. Whether an assistant district attorney, county prosecutor, or city attorney, the prosecutor is typically said to represent the "people" of that jurisdiction. The plaintiff is the party bringing the legal action. The defendant is the one against whom the legal complaint is lodged. In many states, criminal cases are captioned "People of [California] versus John Doe."

In criminal cases, the verdict results in a conviction or an acquittal. If the defendant is acquitted, the matter is ended as our state and federal constitutions prohibit repeated prosecutions for the same offense. If convicted, the defendant faces incarceration, fines, and a host of other rehabilitative or punitive measures.

In civil cases, the most frequent objective of the plaintiff is to recover money, often referred to as damages, for a wrong committed by the defendant, or injury suffered because of the defendant's conduct. A distinct type of civil case, the administrative hearing, is used in DWI cases to determine if a driver should lose his or her driving privileges, temporarily or permanently.

Whether it is a criminal or a civil case, it may be decided by a judge [called a bench trial] or by a jury. In both cases, formal testimony under oath is taken and the same rules of evidence apply. A major distinction between civil and criminal cases involves the burden of proof. In civil cases, the plaintiff must prove he or she is entitled to win by a "preponderance of the evidence." This means the plaintiff must show it is more likely than not that certain facts are true. Some attorneys will use percentages to express this concept and tell juries that if they believe the evidence was 51 percent in support of the fact and 49 percent opposed, they then must find the fact has been successfully proven. In criminal cases, the prosecution must prove the defendant's guilt beyond a reasonable doubt. Though there are no percentage equivalents, everyone concedes that this burden is much higher than in civil cases.

Most cases, whether criminal or civil, settle out of court. In the criminal arena, more than 90 percent of all cases are disposed of through a plea of guilty, a negotiated plea agreement, or rarely, with a dismissal of the charge.

One way in which the conduct of litigation differs today from fifty years ago is in the amount of pre-trial work done by the opposing parties. Today, the parties find out as much as they can about the strengths and weaknesses of a case long before trial. Such investigation is referred to as discovery.

The most common methods of conducting discovery, in both civil and criminal cases, are to send a list of questions, or interrogatories, to the other side, and to conduct depositions. A deposition is the taking of testimony under oath, but outside the trial setting. Typically, the attorneys for both sides are present and a court reporter makes a record of everything said. A judge is almost never present when the deposition is taken.

The purpose of a deposition is to discover what the witness knows that is relevant to the case or to preserve the witness's testimony for later presentation to the judge or jury. Most everything in the following chapters relating to nonverbal and verbal persuasion applies equally to depositions and to testimony given in court. There are some caveats applicable to the deposition process; these are set forth in Chapter Five.

Most trials are heard by juries, rather than by judges sitting without a jury. There are many reasons for this. In the criminal context, judges are generally perceived by the defense bar as too conservative, too unwilling to accept a defense they've seen presented countless times before. One judge, during a break in a DWI jury trial, said, "If I hear the trick-knee excuse for failing the walk-and-turn test one more time, I'm going to be sick." In civil cases, plaintiffs typically believe a jury will award them more money in damages than will a judge.

So, in most cases, you will be attempting to persuade a jury as the finder of fact. Occasionally, the decision-maker will be a judge. But even in jury cases, you will need to impress the judge with your credibility, as it often impacts crucial rulings by the court during the trial. The advice in this book applies regardless of whether your target audience is a jury or the judge.

Section Four: Just the Facts, Ma'am

It may seem obvious that you cannot persuade someone to believe a certain set of facts unless you know them well enough yourself to convey them easily. It should come as no surprise that a jury or judge will view the halting, stammering, unsure witness as less credible than another who exudes confidence by demonstrating familiarity with the facts. This may stem from our knowledge of the human tendency to stall when we don't know the answer or when we wish to fabricate one. The better you know your facts, the easier time you will have fending off attacks on your credibility.

Jurors and judges recognize that some cases are quite complex and a witness may have a thick file full of information related to the case. No one expects you to have a photographic memory. Many witnesses will want to take some notes with them to the witness stand to refresh their memory on certain matters. As will be pointed out in Chapter Three, this is generally a bad idea. At times, however, it may be unavoidable.

In most cases, you should not need, nor should you take notes with you to the witness stand. Instead, take time to read through the file and familiarize yourself with the facts of the case before coming to court. The witness who cannot testify to the most elementary facts without referring to notes sends the judge and jury two messages. First, the witness is not the sharpest knife in the drawer, and, second, the witness did not care much about the matter at hand. Either message may be fatal to the case.

One way of increasing your knowledge of the facts is to have a co-worker, spouse, or friend look over your report. Ask the reviewer to assume the mindset of the attorney on the other side. What issues or areas of the report will most likely be explored by opposing counsel? The more trial-savvy your reviewer is, the better this particular exercise will prepare you for trial. Perhaps the best reviewer and advisor in this regard is your attorney.

It is recognized that you may not have an attorney who specifically represents you in the case. Throughout this book, "prosecuting attorney" and "your attorney" are used interchangeably. While most of your testimony will likely come in the context of a criminal trial, you may also have to testify in a civil lawsuit. For example, you may be called upon to testify in a personal injury suit arising out of an auto collision, a police brutality lawsuit, or at an administrative hearing to revoke the liquor license of a tavern owner. In these civil actions, there won't be a prosecutor. But there will still be an attorney you would more closely align yourself with, given a choice. This attorney is referred to as "your attorney."

The attorney who calls a witness to the stand does the "direct examination" of that witness. The questioning is typically open-ended and not suggestive. The most frequently heard question on direct examination is "What happened next?"

Opposing counsel conducts what is called "cross-examination." On cross-examination, the questioner typically states the facts and merely asks the witness to confirm them. Many questions on cross-examination begin, "Isn't it true that … ?" or "Would you admit that … ?" An adage repeated by trial lawyers is that you never ask a question on cross-examination for which you do not already know the answer.

The attorney who violates this rule tempts fate, as demonstrated by the following story that has made the rounds among trial lawyers:

Cross-examiner:	So you say my client, Mr. Jones, assaulted Mr. Smith.
Witness:	Yes, that's right.
Cross-examiner:	And you say my client did this by biting off Mr. Smith's ear?
Witness:	Correct.
Cross-examiner:	But you admit, don't you, that at the same time this alleged assault took place, a train went by within fifty feet of where you were standing?
Witness:	Yes, that's true.
Cross-examiner:	And you admit you were distracted by the train, correct?
Witness:	Yes.
Cross-examiner:	In fact, at the exact moment the alleged assault took place, you weren't even looking at my client were you?
Witness:	No, I wasn't.
Cross-examiner:	Nor were you looking at Mr. Smith at that time, correct?
Witness:	That's right.
Cross-examiner:	So you couldn't possibly have seen my client commit this so-called assault, could you?
Witness:	No, I guess I couldn't.

[Then comes the question for which the cross-examiner does not know the answer, and, advisedly, should never ask.]

Cross-examiner:	Without committing perjury, how can you possibly testify under oath that my client bit off Mr. Smith's ear?
Witness:	I saw him spit it out.

After your attorney finishes with your direct testimony, opposing counsel conducts cross-examination. Your attorney then is allowed to ask more questions but is limited to the areas covered by opposing counsel on cross-examination; this is called redirect examination. In the judge's discretion, there may follow recross-examination, re-redirect, and so on. The only restriction is that the topics covered must be only those just addressed by the previous examiner. In other words, the cross-examiner cannot wait until recross-examination and then bring up a new subject which wasn't covered on redirect examination.

If the adversary system works as designed, any relevant facts you have will be brought to light by one attorney or the other. The better you know them, the shorter will be your stay on the witness stand.

Section Five: Educating Your Attorney

For an attorney at trial, what you don't know not only can hurt you, it can kill your case. Trial lawyers can tell numerous stories of how they were ambushed in the courtroom by the revelation of some fact previously unknown to them. This occurrence is so common, law school trial advocacy instructors advise students of the importance of appearing nonchalant when the bombshell explodes in open court. "Whatever you do," they instruct, "don't appear to be surprised or flustered by the revelation. To do so only emphasizes its importance to the jury. Pretend it was insignificant and hope for the best."

A prosecutor may have a good idea what kind of defense will be put on and can prepare for it. What the prosecutor can't prepare for are those facts which you hold in your head but have not divulged. There are many reasons why a witness may choose not to tell the attorney everything the witness knows about a particular event. The most common is the belief that the information will hurt the case and is better left unstated. Acting on this rationale by concealing information is particularly dangerous in the legal arena and is unlikely to succeed. Under modern discovery rules, the opposing attorney is likely to uncover the harmful evidence unless people dishonestly cover it up. Even then, it seems that over time, the truth is revealed. When this happens, opposing counsel can seek a new trial alleging newly discovered evidence.

Concealment is a risky approach; if it backfires and the previously undisclosed evidence is adduced at trial, there is little time to diminish its impact or contradict it. Most trials are relatively short. Even murder trials seldom last longer than two or three weeks in most states. Unsurprisingly, one dramatic revelation of a pertinent fact is easily remembered by jurors at trial's end when they begin deliberating.

Witnesses sometimes choose not to "educate" their attorney assuming, erroneously, it is unnecessary. Almost all attorneys in the United States earn a bachelor's degree before attending law school. Then there are three more years of rigorous study. Lawyers are a bright group of people. Law schools, however, do not require any particular area of undergraduate study as a prerequisite for admission. Many of my law school classmates majored in political science; others concentrated their studies in such varied disciplines as biology, French, theology, and engineering.

Your attorney may know little or nothing about accident reconstruction, breathalyzer operation, or other subjects you know well. You have expertise by virtue of your education, training, and experience. You need to share as much of it as you can, given time constraints, with your attorney, insofar as it relates to the subject of your testimony. It is far better that you be too thorough than to omit something.

Section Six: Know the Battleground

If anxiety makes witnesses appear unsure of themselves, tense, and otherwise less credible than they should be, part of any stress reduction plan includes witness familiarity with the courtroom setting, the "battleground," if you will. You need to know where this search for the truth, this civilized battle will take place. Fortunately, our courthouses and courtrooms are generally accessible to the public.

Tip #1: Visit the courtroom

There is no reason why you can't or shouldn't visit a courtroom, preferably the one where you will later testify, before trial. Go to the courthouse and ask to speak to the court administrator. Explain your purpose and ask for permission to visit the courtroom. Unless it is in use, most court administrators will accommodate you. When you get there, look around. Where is the witness stand? Sometimes people confuse the witness stand with the place where a clerk of court or a court stenographer sits. Take a seat on the witness stand. How easy is it for you to see the judge, jury box, and tables where the attorneys will sit?

In the best of all worlds, the prosecutor will make the arrangements for your courtroom visit and accompany you. Ask the prosecutor how the oath is administered to witnesses in this judge's court. Is it done by the bailiff? A clerk? The judge? It can be unnerving to walk into a room full of strangers and not know where to stand, who to address, or what to do. Witnesses face this scenario daily.

Back on the witness stand, try out the sound system (almost all courtrooms use microphones and amplification so witnesses, attorneys, and the judge can be easily heard). If the system is turned off, don't be afraid to walk up to the judge's chair where the sound system controls typically are found. Turn it on.

Adjust your distance from the microphone in order to achieve the desired volume. It is unlikely anyone will fine-tune the system during trial to accommodate loud and soft witnesses. Any adjustments must be made by you. Be aware that the microphone may not pick up your voice when you lean back in your chair and that you may come across too loudly if you get too close to the microphone.

Tip #2: Understand the chronology of a trial

Ask the prosecutor what will happen in court on the day you will testify. The course of a typical trial is this:

1. Prospective jurors are questioned by the judge and attorneys and some of them are selected to serve on the jury. In most civil cases, juries consist of nine jurors. In felony criminal cases, the standard is twelve jurors, while many misdemeanor criminal cases are heard by six jurors. The numbers may vary from state to state. The jury selection process is called "voir dire" which means "to speak the truth." Voir dire may take anywhere from an hour to several days to complete.
2. The judge may give the newly empaneled jury some opening instructions.
3. Attorneys make opening statements. The prosecution or plaintiff in a civil case always goes first. The defendant's attorney then gives an opening statement. The defense may, but rarely does, reserve opening statement until the plaintiff's case has been presented.
4. The plaintiff calls witnesses to testify.
5. The plaintiff rests.
6. The defendant calls witnesses to testify. The defendant in all criminal cases and in most civil cases is not required to present any evidence. A defendant does not have to call a single witness. The "burden of proof" is always on the plaintiff to prove the defendant has violated the law or is otherwise answerable to the plaintiff's claim. In most criminal cases, the defendant does not testify.
7. The defendant rests.
8. The plaintiff may call rebuttal witnesses.

9. The plaintiff again rests.
10. Attorneys make closing arguments. The plaintiff argues first and has the right to make a rebuttal argument after the defendant has argued.
11. The judge gives closing instructions to the jury. Some judges, by custom or rule, give closing jury instructions before the attorneys make closing arguments.
12. The jury retires to deliberate on a verdict.
13. The jury returns with a verdict and it is announced in open court.
14. In criminal cases, the defendant is acquitted and can leave, or is convicted and may be sentenced immediately or after a pre-sentence investigation has been conducted.

For reasons set out in Chapter Two, you will want to know if you are coming to court on the same day the jury is selected. You may also want to know if you will be testifying first, last, or somewhere in the middle of the pack. Ask your attorney.

Section Seven: Techniques to Reduce Anxiety

Tip #1: Go through a dry run

The best preparation you can make for testifying is to have your attorney take you through a dry run. The attorney should put you on the witness stand and ask you the very questions that will be asked at trial, offering critiques as you go along. When done with direct examination, the attorney should assume the role of the cross-examining attorney and ask you questions that defense counsel is likely to ask.

This will give you a good idea of how the questioning will proceed when you're called upon to do the real thing. But is it ethical? Some witnesses have asked if it is proper to go over your testimony in advance of trial. The short answer is an unequivocal "Yes." It is not only ethical, it is encouraged.

An attorney who is well prepared for trial will have conducted dry runs, or at a minimum, given witnesses a list of questions the attorney intends to ask on direct examination. Some attorneys, after interviewing the witness and reviewing pertinent reports, will send each witness a list of questions and anticipated responses to those questions. The list is typically accompanied by a caveat to the effect that the enclosed responses are based on information received from the witness previously and that if any of the anticipated responses are incomplete or inaccurate, the witness should contact the attorney to discuss them.

Every attorney has an ethical obligation to refrain from presenting perjured testimony. But attorneys are also required to represent their clients zealously. This means that, so long as the answers are truthful, attorneys and witnesses are free to rehearse them before trial.

But what if opposing counsel attempts to impugn your integrity with questions about your rehearsal? If your attorney has prepared you well, the questioning may go like this:

Cross-examiner:	Is it true, Mr. Jones, that you have met with the prosecutor, Mr. Oatfield, to discuss this case?
Witness:	Yes.
Cross-examiner:	You've met with him several times?
Witness:	Yes.
Cross-examiner:	And the two of you discussed the testimony you've just given us, isn't that true?
Witness:	Yes, that's true.
Cross-examiner:	[Accusingly] In fact, you came into this very courtroom, sat in this same witness chair, and went over your story, didn't you?
Witness:	Yes.
Cross-examiner:	[Smugly] No further questions for this witness.

Prosecutor:	May I ask just a few more questions, your honor?
Judge:	Yes, you may.
Prosecutor:	Mr. Smith, do you remember the first time we discussed the fact that you would probably have to testify in court?
Witness:	I remember, yes.
Prosecutor:	There was something I told you that day that I said was more important than anything else. Do you remember what that was?
Witness:	Yes. You said to tell the truth, no matter what.
Prosecutor:	And that's what you have done today?
Witness:	Absolutely.
Prosecutor:	[Justifiably smug] Thank you. Nothing further.

Knowing where you will be and how trials progress will lessen the anxiety of testifying in court. Once you have been inside the courtroom and heard some of the questions that will be asked when you actually take the witness stand you are ready to engage in one further means of preparation.

Tip #2: Use imagery

Imagery is the process of imagining through any sense: hearing, sight, smell, taste, or touch. It has sometimes been called psycho-cybernetics or visualization. Imagery has been used since ancient times as a technique to encourage changes in attitudes, behavior, or physiological reactions. It is used in a wide variety of therapies and may also be used as a form of meditation. Health care professionals have demonstrated through scientific studies that imagery can affect a number of physiological functions, including brain-wave activity, blood glucose levels, cardiovascular function, gastrointestinal activity, and oxygen supply in tissues.

Coaches have long recognized the importance of imagery, also called visualization by some, in preparing athletes for competition. One swimming coach wrote:

> To perform well in a big meet, you have to 'experience' the whole thing in advance! This means you must 'feel' the atmosphere of the big occasion, 'see' your competitors, the coaches, the pool, and your friends, 'smell' the water, 'hear' the crowd—I could go on and on, you have to immerse yourself into the entire meet if you want to be truly prepared for it. If you do not do this, you can find yourself becoming overwhelmed on the day by the big occasion. This is exactly what so many swimmers do—they train brilliantly all week and then get stressed out at the meets and do not perform at their best.[1]

A martial arts expert advises his students to:

1. Visualize yourself executing a technique with perfect balance, accuracy, and coordination.
2. Imagine how to react to a specific self-defense situation. Visualize your opponent or attacker delivering a front kick or right cross. Think about how you should react. See yourself reacting confidently with strong counters and strikes.
3. Create a strong visualization for greater impact. Use all of your senses to observe the detail of sensations, such as the feel and movement of a kick, the texture of your uniform, and the sounds of your feet moving.
4. Imagine yourself within your body rather than looking at yourself from a distance. It creates a more realistic visualization.
5. Anticipate the anxiety and stress that comes with competition and promotion testing. Visualize yourself using deep-breathing techniques and performing confidently to reduce your stress level.[2]

All proponents of imagery advise that you begin the process by finding a quiet place to sit or lie down. Relax muscle groups of your body by tensing them for five seconds and then letting them go. Start with your feet and work your way up the body. By the time you've flexed and released your facial muscles, your body and mind should be more receptive to the imagery exercise.

As with athletic contests, imagine the setting. Yours will not be a swimming pool or gymnasium, but a courtroom. "See" the attorneys, jurors, clerk of court, judge, and perhaps some people in the audience watching the whole thing. Remember the ambiance of the place, the color of the carpet and woodwork. "Hear" the official administer the oath. "Feel" what it's like to sit in the chair on the witness stand, adjusting the microphone, and listening to how your first answer comes across the public address system.

Then imagine yourself being cool, calm, and collected. In your mind, see yourself as an unflappable witness speaking to the jurors as if they were interested neighbors and friends clinging to every word you utter. Visualize a confident, smooth delivery with just the right amount of inflection and a serious tone to your voice. Picture yourself handling cross-examination with measured, matter-of-fact responses. Then see yourself thanking the judge, stepping down from the witness stand and walking confidently out of the courtroom.

There, you've done it! Your body will associate the calm you are experiencing in your resting, imaging setting with the mental environment of the courtroom you have created. Believe it or not, your brain cannot distinguish this "dry run" from the real thing. If you repeat the imaging exercise, when it comes time to actually testify, you will enter the courtroom with the confidence that you've "been there, done that." Give it a try. Believe me. It works!

Chapter Two

What You Need to Know at Trial

Section One: Nonverbal Persuasion

Judge:	You may call your next witness.
Prosecutor:	We call Mary Smith.

If you have been seated outside the courtroom, a bailiff or the prosecutor will call you to take the witness stand. When you enter the courtroom, it may well be the first time the jury and judge see you. You have only one opportunity to make a good first impression. For good or ill, people judge us by our appearance. Assumptions are made about our status and credibility based solely on how we look. Even though those assumptions and first impressions may be, and often are, wrong, you should not create unnecessary hurdles that must be overcome by your testimony.

Tip #1: Avoid jewelry

As a general rule, the less jewelry you wear, the better. If you are married, you should definitely wear a wedding ring, assuming it is not ostentatious. You don't want to blind the jury with the light reflecting from your huge diamond ring. Leave the other rings at home. The same is true for bracelets, necklaces, and earrings. Men should not wear them at all in the courtroom, and women should wear necklaces or earrings only if they do not command attention. Do not wear bracelets on your ankles or wrists.

Be mindful of wearing anything that looks too expensive. Someone on the jury may have a bias against rich people and be turned off by that beautiful Rolex watch. ("On *my* salary? You've got to be kidding!") Although your role as a witness has some of the trappings of a performance, you should not look like you're a star.

Tip #2: Dress professionally

At one time, I would have urged witnesses to dress as if they were going to church. But with today's relaxed standard, that probably is no longer safe advice. I've seen fellow parishioners wearing jeans and tank tops to service, definitely inappropriate attire for the witness stand.

Anyone who customarily wears a uniform to work should wear it on the witness stand as well. The uniform evokes authority, which is desirable. You may be off-duty when you testify in court. Nevertheless, you should wear your uniform, if you have one. It is a good idea to have it cleaned and pressed. If your uniform includes a hat, wear it, but remove it as you enter the courtroom. Tuck it under your arm. It is part of your official dress and there is no good reason to leave it outside the courtroom.

If you do not normally wear a uniform, you need to maintain the image of a professional. James Rasicot, a psychologist, studied the impact dress has on credibility. He had actors recite the same testimony in a mock trial setting while wearing different sets of clothes. He then asked several groups of mock jurors to rate the actors on credibility, that is, grade them on how believable they were. The results were illuminating, though not surprising. They could best be summarized this way: the more conservative the attire, the more authoritative and credible the witness was perceived as being.

For men, the most credible witness was one who wore a dark suit with a white shirt and red tie. The least credible witness was one who wore jeans and a T-shirt. Persons wearing a sport coat, colored shirt, and tie were viewed as more credible than someone wearing slacks and a sport shirt, but less credible than one wearing a suit.[3]

Solid colors or pinstripes are fine; plaids are not. John T. Molloy, in his book, *Dress For Success,* says, "There are only three appropriate colors for men in a business setting—'dull, dark and drab.'"[4]

For women, wearing a three-piece suit with a white blouse proved to be the most credibility-enhancing attire. A low-cut neckline connotes someone out to impress with her body, not her mind. A tailored, as opposed to loose-fitting, look is more authoritative. Solid colors are preferred to mixed, and dark colors are generally preferable to bright ones. Wearing shoes with heels, not spikes, gives an air of sophistication while wearing flats does not. Women who put their hair up and pull it away from the face look more powerful than those who do not.

For both men and women, wearing glasses connotes you read more and are more intelligent than those who don't wear them. So if you have contact lenses, leave them at home and wear your glasses to court. Shoes should be polished, clothes cleaned and pressed. If you wear a tie, make sure it is of modern width and pattern. You don't have to be a fashion plate or wear the trendiest clothes, but you won't impress anyone wearing your grandfather's suspenders and a too-wide, stained tie. Pretend it's a job interview and you want to make your best impression.

If you have tattoos that are easily concealed by clothing, do so. While tattoos are far more popular today than in the past, for many older citizens they connote a host of bad attributes. Men with tattoos may be viewed as sleazy, dirty, crooked, and untrustworthy, while women may be viewed as promiscuous, vain, or disrespectful. Never mind that these stereotypes are largely false. Most juries are composed of older people. Since they are the ones calling the shots, making the ultimate decision in your case, it does no good to alienate them if it can be avoided.

Any hair style, makeup, or clothing that calls attention away from the substance of your testimony should be avoided. You need the jury and judge to be able to easily concentrate on what you say.

Tip #3: How to take the stand

Judge:	You may call your next witness, counsel.
Attorney Jones:	We call John Doe to the stand.

All attention shifts to the courtroom door where the bailiff exits to summon you to testify. Seconds later you enter and walk to the witness stand. Having visited the courtroom in advance, you know exactly where you're going. You stride confidently to the front of the courtroom where the clerk of court administers the oath to you. In those few seconds, the jury gets its first glimpse of you and immediately the jurors begin to assess your credibility. What are they looking for as they size you up? Posture and evenness of your gait are two important factors. The advice every mother gives her teenage child is appropriate: "Stand tall, walk erect, don't slouch."

If you walk without hesitation and hold your head high, the jury will see a confident person for whom they will immediately have respect. You will not disappoint them.

Tip #4: Taking the oath

The standard oath is, "Do you swear that your testimony will be the truth, the whole truth, and nothing but the truth, so help you God?" There are slight variations in some courts, of course. Some witnesses, generally for religious reasons, prefer not to swear an oath. Most courts will allow an alternative oath along these lines to be given, "Do you promise, under pain of perjury, to tell the truth in these proceedings?" If you want the alternative oath, simply tell the person administering the oath that you prefer not to "swear." They will know what to do.

You should ask your attorney in advance who will be administering the oath to you at trial. It varies from court to court. It may be the judge, a clerk of court, the court reporter, or a bailiff. If you know the party who will give you the oath, you can approach him or her without having to look to others for direction. Again, this exhibition of courtroom knowledge is likely to impress jurors with your competence.

When you approach the oath administrator, raise your right hand without prompting. Answer the oath query with a firm, audible "I do" or "I will." Then turn and take the witness stand. Before you sit down, it is a good idea to wait for the judge to tell you to be seated. No one will chastise you if you do not wait, but pausing for a second or two shows the judge and the jury that you respect the judge's authority.

Though many attorneys wish it weren't so, jurors identify with the judge far more often and more closely than they do with any of the attorneys. If there is a disagreement in front of the jury, it is the rare case where jurors side with the attorney. The judge, on the other hand, typically treats the jury with respect. Jurors frequently view the judge and jury working as a team, trying to reach the best decision in the case.

You tap into this natural camaraderie by showing deference to the judge. Regardless of your personal opinion of the person wearing the black robe, showing courtesy and respect for the position of judge will only enhance your credibility in the eyes of both the judge and jury.

Tip #5: Maintain a "powerful" posture on the witness stand

James Rasicot also studied the effects of posture on witness credibility. His research again supported mom's advice: "Sit up, don't slouch." In general, Rasicot concluded, the more space you take up when standing or sitting, the more powerful you are perceived as being. Power, he noted, enhances credibility. So, within reason, assume a posture that uses more space rather than less. That means that if you sit stoop-shouldered or hunched forward, you will be perceived as less credible than if you sit erectly.

Both feet should be on the floor. Arms should be at your side, not draped over the back of the chair or resting with your hands more than a few inches apart. You do not want to give the impression that these proceedings are informal or unimportant. A sprawling appearance tells the jury you lack self-discipline or are insensitive to social norms.

Don't cross your legs or arms. Crossing your legs indicates an informality generally foreign to the courtroom. Crossed arms send the signal that you are smug or unwilling to openly discuss whatever issue has led to this nonverbal response on your part. Good attorneys will take note of the psychological discomfort that caused the crossed-arms response. It's like waving a red flag at them. As soon as the attorney notes the arms crossing or the body shifting away from the attorney, a question comes immediately to mind: "Why is this person so anxious about this particular subject?" The attorney then silently concludes, "I think this area deserves further attention."

Your objective is to keep cross-examination as short and painless as possible. If, through your body language, you prod opposing counsel to keep you on the stand longer in order to question you about a subject that evidently causes you anxiety, it rarely works to your advantage.

Tip #6: Avoid indicators of deception

Many of us have had the experience of questioning a child about a broken object or some missing cookies. When the youngster's face flushes and the eyes dart, we know the child's response may be something less than truthful.

A retired FBI agent who specialized in interrogations of criminals conducted a training session where he taught attendees to look for the "indicators of deception" when interviewing suspects. The following list of such indicators is representative, though not all-inclusive:

Rubbing or wringing of hands

Scratching yourself

Pulling on earlobes or nose

Stroking or grooming hair

Inspecting or picking fingernails

Adjusting clothing

Taking eyeglasses off or cleaning them

Picking lint or pulling threads from clothing

Putting hand to back of head or neck

Wiping lips or eyes

Shuffling, tapping, or swinging feet

Probing ears or nose

Shifting leg posture or alignment coinciding with pertinent questions

Wiping sweat

Feet locked together under chair

Lack of frontal alignment

Removing or adjusting watches or jewelry

Rhythmic drumming of fingers

Closed body position with arms and elbows particularly close to the body

Hiding of mouth and/or eyes

These deception indicators arise from the unconscious need to relieve anxiety and reduce stress through some motor activity. When a suspect engages in the deceptive conduct, interrogators makes a note to explore that area in greater detail. In the courtroom, attorneys are like interrogators looking for particular subjects that may be probed to help their case. Indicators of deception help the watchful attorney narrow the focus of cross-examination.

While not all anxiety, especially in a courtroom, is induced by telling a falsehood, most people interpret the stress-reducing behavior as indicative of lying on the stand. Therefore, "appearance is reality." If jurors *think* you're lying, it doesn't make much difference whether or not you are testifying truthfully.

Do judges and jurors really know when you're not telling the truth? There is some research which shows judges were accurate only half of the time when guessing which witness statements were truthful and which were fabricated. But another study supports the hypothesis that all of us have a built-in lie detector.

Aphasics are people who do not understand the meaning of words but can still communicate because they gather meaning from nonverbal cues. One researcher found aphasics were particularly adept at recognizing lies from the speaker's tone, emphasis, facial expression, and gestures. If aphasics have this ability, the rest of us most probably possess it too, though we may not recognize it.[5] In short, jurors probably have a subconscious feel for whether or not a witness is lying, based on body language and speech inflection. The trouble is, your body language, while indicative of lying, may simply be the result of nervousness.

You need to be comfortable on the witness stand. That comfort level will rise with experience and with the knowledge of how jurors perceive you. Going through a "dry run" and using imagery will reduce anxiety and lessen the chance that you will unwittingly exhibit indicators of deception. So will learning what to expect in court.

Tip #7: Be comfortable with a microphone

Most courtrooms today have sound systems, that is, microphones, amplifiers and speakers. Jurors with hearing disabilities may be given a special apparatus that allows them to better hear words spoken into the microphones in court. And therein lies the key to effective communication. You must use the sound system to your full advantage. As noted earlier, if you have the opportunity to visit the courtroom before trial, by all means do so. Ask your lawyer to turn on the sound system so you can hear how your voice sounds in the room.

If you do not get the opportunity to rehearse with the sound system before trial, calmly sit down, make brief eye contact with the judge and jury, then look to your attorney for the first question. The question, almost invariably, is "Would you state your name for the record, please?" When you respond, *listen* to how your voice is amplified and adjust your distance from the microphone accordingly.

Jurors won't mind if the first few words come blasting out at them so long as you move away from the microphone from then on. But if you continually "eat the mike"—speak too closely to the microphone—the loud sound will be abrasive enough that the judge will probably tell you to back off.

A worse problem, and one more frequently encountered, is the soft voice. Women are more prone than men to speak inaudibly but I've heard testimony from many soft-spoken men who were difficult to understand. Your attorney will usually let you know if you are not coming across loudly enough but you should be able to gauge this without help. Look to the jury to see if they are following your testimony.

Remember, your words may carry all the wisdom of Solomon but they will do your cause no good if the jury and judge can't hear them. This is common sense, of course, but you would be amazed at the number of witnesses whose testimony is undervalued because they do not "speak up." Nor do jurors appreciate the attorney who must constantly advise a witness to speak more loudly.

A moderately loud voice also indicates confidence. Jurors favor confident witnesses and view them as more credible than those appearing less confident.

Tip #8: Make eye contact

Generally speaking, maintaining good eye contact with your listeners is a good method of increasing credibility. It helps establish rapport and assures your audience of your sincerity. Lawyers know this and, if the judge allows it, often stand at the corner of the jury box while questioning an important witness. This requires the witness to look at or at least look in the general direction of the jurors while testifying.

I once prosecuted a divorced father for molesting his five- and six-year-old daughters during a weekend visitation. There was scant physical evidence. The father adamantly denied fondling the girls. Worse, a judge allowed the visitations to continue even after the charges were filed and, sure enough, the girls recanted. In other words, they "changed their story" and told a social worker that the fondling never happened.

This kind of case is a prosecutor's nightmare, but I was fortunate to have as one of my witnesses Joan Senzek Solheim. Joan had impeccable credentials as a child psychologist, having been trained at the world-renowned Kemp Institute in Denver, Colorado. She had studied child sexual abuse extensively and worked with hundreds of abused children. I wanted Joan to explain to the jury the phenomenon of "recanting" and what it meant, or rather, what it did not mean. She took the witness stand and looked at me directly as she answered preliminary questions about her education and experience. But when I got to the crucial question, the one that asked her to explain recantation in children, her body shifted. She turned thirty degrees or so in the witness chair so that she was facing the jury directly. Then, with confidence and skill, she looked at each juror in turn as she explained that children often recant when faced with unpleasant repercussions from their earlier statement. It did not mean the sexual abuse did not happen.

Her explanation took three or four minutes. I watched in awe as she nonverbally contacted each juror assuring them of her sincerity. She meant every word she said and she wanted them to know it. They did. I could see that Joan had them eating out of the palm of her hand. When she was done, I wanted to stand up and applaud her, she was that good. The jury convicted.

In another case, a smooth-talking salesman was accused of fraud. He sold coin-operated blood pressure machines, telling customers he would place them in high-traffic areas, and they would reap the profits. The problem was, he sold more machines than he owned. His customers were mostly elderly, naive, and trusting. He bilked them of thousands of dollars.

When the salesman took the stand at trial, he had answers for everything. His attorney must have spent more than two hours asking him questions designed to show the efficacy of the sales scheme. What struck me as odd was that not once, in his two hours of direct examination and twenty minutes on cross-examination, did the defendant look at the jury. Not once. He was a scam artist and I believe the jury spotted him right away. He was convicted after a short deliberation.

There is no rule that says when you testify you have to look at opposing counsel while being cross-examined. If the question allows you to give anything but a "yes" or "no" answer, you are free to turn to the jury and tell them forthrightly whatever you can honestly say in answer to the query. Pick your moment, though. It looks a bit awkward if you turn to the jury after being asked questions that require only a brief answer, i.e., "How long have you been in law enforcement?" [turn, face jury] "Seven years." [turn back, face attorney]

Although sustained eye contact is usually viewed favorably by the recipient when judging your credibility, you should be aware that, as in all things human, there are exceptions. For example, numerous researchers have found that among certain segments of the population, eye contact is sometimes viewed as disrespectful or implying arrogance. According to the research, cultures most commonly associated with these beliefs are Asian, Pacific Islander, and Native American.[6]

With regard to Native Americans, my experience has not borne out this observation. I have seen, talked to, examined, and cross-examined hundreds of Native Americans on reservations in the Dakotas. Included among them were members of the Lakota, Cheyenne, Mandan, Arikara, Hidatsa, and Chippewa tribes. I have yet to see any adverse reaction from them to solid eye contact. When I have raised the issue with some Native American friends, they uniformly denied there is any stigma attached to normal or sustained eye contact. I caution to add there are hundreds of tribes in the United States and my experience may not be universal.

It is always wise to take your cues from your listener. If you notice a juror avert your eye contact, don't linger and make him or her uncomfortable. Let common sense be your guide.

Section Two: Be Aware of Other Nonverbal Factors Affecting Your Credibility

Distractions

You have one chance and one chance only to educate the jury. That means you must take advantage of the opportunity by doing everything in your power to keep the jury's attention focused on you throughout your testimony. Anything that distracts jurors from the message you hope to convey diminishes your chances of persuading them.

Some things most people find distracting include chewing gum, rattling coins in your pocket, or fumbling with papers in a file while talking. Women should not take a purse to the stand. Men should empty their pockets before going into the courtroom. Leave behind your cell phone and anything else that makes noise or is visually distracting to your audience. They need to concentrate on what you are saying and how you are saying it.

Looking to the Lawyer

Although your attorney can help you through adept questioning and objections to some questions put to you by opposing counsel, for the most part you are on your own while on the witness stand. Your attorney can't give you hints on how to answer tough questions. So when faced with a particularly hard question from the other side, don't make the mistake of looking to your attorney for help.

If the jury sees this, and they will, your credibility will take a nose dive. A witness who can't answer truthfully without assistance can't be trusted, they will surely surmise. At a minimum, the jury may infer that you are looking for help because you are unsure of yourself.

Sometimes, you can get a little breathing room by asking opposing counsel to rephrase the question. "I'm sorry. I don't understand your question. Could you ask it again, please? or "I'm not sure what you're asking. Could you rephrase your question, please?" If you are polite and the tactic is not abused, you may gain a few precious seconds which may allow you to compose your answer. But if you use the ploy more than once, a jury may see it as an attempt to avoid telling the truth.

Sequestration

There is a rule of evidence followed in most courts called the "sequestration rule." The gist of it is this. If any party wants witnesses kept out of the courtroom until they testify, the party simply needs to ask the judge and the request must be granted. The judge will say something like this: "Pursuant to Rule 615 of the Rules of Evidence, I am ordering all witnesses to leave the courtroom and to remain outside until the bailiff calls you. You are also directed not to confer with anyone about the testimony given in this courtroom before such time as you testify yourself."

Your attorney should inform you whether or not the sequestration rule has been invoked so that you are not embarrassed by being ordered to leave the courtroom. If the rule has not been invoked, you may want to listen to the testimony given by other witnesses.

Even if the rule is in effect, you are usually permitted to remain in the courtroom while opening statements are made and, generally, it is a good idea to listen while the opposition outlines their theory of the case. But once the first witness takes the stand, I would recommend you not be in the courtroom except when testifying. You can catch a blow-by-blow description of the events from your attorney at the end of the day or when the trial is over. Moreover, the time to learn what other witnesses are expected to say on the witness stand is before the trial. Ask your attorney what others are anticipated to say while testifying. This is proper.

If you are sequestered, most courts hold that you must stay out of the courtroom before *and* after you testify if there is any chance that you may be called back to the stand as a rebuttal witness. Only if your attorney assures the judge that you will not be recalled are you free to stay. Again, it may be to your advantage not to stay in the courtroom after testifying even if it is permissible.

When opposing counsel says, "No further questions, Your Honor," the judge will usually say, "Thank you, Ms. Anderson; you may step down." On occasion, your attorney or opposing counsel will ask the court for permission to recall you as a witness. "Your Honor, I may want to call Ms. Anderson as a rebuttal witness." In this event, the judge will probably advise you that you are still subject to the sequestration rule, meaning that you should not discuss the case with anyone until the trial is over or you've been assured you will not be recalled as a witness.

But in most cases, when you step down from the witness stand, your part in the trial is completed. So what should you do? I suggest you nod to the judge, say "Thank you, Your Honor," and walk confidently to the exit. Go out and don't return unless summoned by the court or your attorney. On your way out, avoid eye contact with the attorneys, jurors, or anyone at counsel table. Do not look at the prosecutor for verbal or nonverbal cues. If there's information the prosecutor wants you to have, you'll get it. Any nod or smile exchanged between you will be noticed. Just look straight ahead and leave.

Why not take a seat in the audience? Surely you're interested in the outcome. Even if you weren't, trials can be truly fascinating to watch. Don't succumb to the temptation. The reason for this is simple. One or more of the jurors will note where you are sitting. When another witness makes a bold statement on the stand, jurors may look to you for a reaction. And despite your best intentions, you may convey nonverbally the reaction they're watching for. And it can be a lose-lose situation. If you listen to the testimony of someone who, in your opinion, is being less than truthful, and you react nonverbally with a look of disgust, a juror may wonder if you are trying to influence the witness or the jury. If you don't react, another juror may assume you believe the witness's testimony. If you read a book or magazine in the courtroom, jurors will wonder why you are not engaged in the proceedings; it may be boring to you but for most of them it is a once-in-a-lifetime experience. They may not readily understand why you aren't more interested in the proceedings.

Because you are a public employee, some jurors will wonder why you are hanging around a courtroom when you are being paid to be doing something else. I've had jurors tell me they were displeased with an officer who watched the trial after testifying. "I pay taxes to get a day's work for a day's pay. He should have been out chasing crooks." Never mind that it was probably the officer's day off work and he was in court without pay. You can't win.

When you simply leave the courtroom, you don't open yourself to criticism or speculation about your motives. You want to be viewed as someone who is simply relating the facts as they happened not as a legal vigilante determined to "get your man." You need not be concerned that jurors will forget your testimony if you don't remain in the courtroom as a constant reminder. Your attorney will refresh the jury's collective memory with the crucial aspects of your testimony during closing argument.

Just walk out confident that you have done your best to convince the jury of the facts. Trust the system to do its job. It will, at least in most cases. Above all, don't look surprised when the judge directs you to leave the courtroom under the "sequestration rule," or, worse yet, argue with the judge about your right as a citizen to observe all public proceedings. It is not an argument that will carry the day.

Jury Observation

A corollary to the advice about sequestration is that you should assume you are always in the jury's view. From the time you circle the courthouse parking lot looking for a space until the time when the jury returns its verdict, you may be "watched" by one or more jurors. If two heads are better than one, then twelve sets of eyes perceive much more than most of us imagine. A case of disorderly conduct demonstrates the point [I've altered the names but the events are real]:

Mary Jones worked for an apiarist moving bee hives from field to field. It was hard, physical work and to make matters worse, Mary's boss, George Smith, made unwanted overtures to her and was often rude in his comments to her. George, in his late fifties, was overweight, married, and not attractive to Mary in any way.

One day as they were traveling down a bumpy country road, George made a comment about the firmness of her breasts since they "don't bounce up and down much on this road." To save her job, Mary did her best to ignore him, but a more dramatic incident moved her to take action.

Mary was driving the company truck to work on a sunny morning and pulled down the sun visor to shield her eyes. Something dropped in her lap that almost made her lose control of the vehicle. It was a photograph of a nude overweight man masturbating in front of a mirror. The photo was cropped at the neck but Mary knew whose body it was. Infuriated, Mary didn't report to work but came to my office to press charges.

I was a county prosecutor at the time. A few months later, George stood trial on a charge of disorderly conduct. During the trial, Mary testified to several incidents of sexual harassment. George took the stand and denied them all. Then George's attorney called George's wife, Patricia, to testify. She told the jury that she and George had been happily married for more than thirty years, had a most satisfactory love life, and that George was not the kind of man who would ever do such things.

I called Mary back to the stand as a rebuttal witness. In the course of that direct examination, Mary said that George had referred to her as "Poopsie." Unbeknownst to me at the time, Mary's revelation of the nickname "Poopsie" must have struck a chord with Patricia. Patricia and George had been seated immediately next to one another at the defense table throughout the trial. I later learned from one of the jurors that George often rested his hand on Patricia's leg, just above the knee. When Patricia heard Mary mention "Poopsie," Patricia forcefully took George's hand off her leg and slammed it down on his own thigh. Not a word was spoken, but the jurors, at least several of them, "heard" a message that could not have been more clear. They convicted George in less than thirty minutes, a record in my county.

In another case, a murderer confessed long before trial and was left with only one defense, insanity. As one of the prosecutors, I distrusted the testimony of the defendant's foster mother, Sunni Day, when she described the defendant as a good, clean-cut young man when he lived with her. Something about her seemed disingenuous but I couldn't put my finger on it.

After the guilty verdict was returned, I followed my customary practice of talking to all of the jurors who were willing to discuss the trial. I believed then, and still do, that to improve your trial skills you need to get an honest critique from someone in the "audience." A juror told me that during the trial he came back to court early from the luncheon recess one day. There, to his surprise, the defendant and Sunni Day were standing together in a corridor. A deputy sheriff stood nearby. The defendant and Sunni were engaged in a lengthy kiss. It wasn't the sort of embrace typical of a mother and son. The incident only solidified the juror's view that the defendant was an imposter as well as a murderer.

My point is, jurors do not miss much, if anything, that goes on around them. As a prosecutor, my attention was focused entirely on the witness. Jurors take in much more of their environment.

Before trial starts, you may be subpoenaed to come to the courthouse. You may have to wait while the jury is selected. At this point, no one knows who among the several citizens summoned for jury duty will finally sit on the jury. Everyone you meet in the hall may be a juror.

After voir dire, or jury selection, you may encounter a juror returning to the courthouse from lunch or after an evening at home. Contrary to popular belief, jurors are seldom forced to stay together outside the courtroom until they begin deliberations. In short, there are endless opportunities to "bump into" a juror during trial. The longer the trial, the greater the odds this will happen.

Even when the jurors are in the jury box and you are outside the courtroom, you cannot assume that your conduct will not make its way back to the jury. Often, a friend or relative of a juror will come to court to observe events. If the court takes a recess, the observation (of you) made by this friend or relative may later be conveyed to a juror.

Judges routinely admonish jurors not to talk with anyone about the case during recesses or when they go home at night. But take my word for it, the admonition does not prevent information from being exchanged. Most jurors do not deliberately break the rules, but neither do they turn a deaf ear to someone who has a juicy bit of information about the "star" witness for the prosecution, you! Act accordingly.

Weapons

In most courthouses, there are metal detectors and you won't be allowed to take your firearm into the building. But security measures vary greatly, even within the same state. Some judges don't mind if law enforcement officers wear a sidearm in court. I know one judge who "packs" a pistol in court himself! You should be aware, though, that many judges absolutely forbid weapons in their courtrooms with the possible exception of that carried by the bailiff or security officer on duty. Their fear is not unfounded. On more than one occasion, desperate men have grabbed a weapon from an officer's holster and wounded people in court.

You need to check with someone who is familiar with the judge's practice before taking a firearm into court. If you can't determine the prevailing policy, err on the side of leaving your weapon at home or somewhere safe outside the courtroom. You do not want to be embarrassed in front of the jury when some judge commands you, in an indignant voice, to leave the courtroom and not return until the weapon is secured.

Examining Exhibits

It is possible, even likely, that you will serve as the conduit for the introduction of some exhibit at trial. Without you, the document or object will not become part of the evidence for the judge or jury to consider. In order to get the exhibit admitted into evidence, the attorney who wants to have it admitted must first get the judge's authorization. To do this, the proponent usually must lay a proper foundation.

If you took a piece of evidence into custody, you most likely placed it in an evidence bag, marked it with your initials, indicated the time and date of the activity, and sealed it. When you review the exhibit at trial, you should be sure that your initials are on it. Also check to see if the seal has been broken. If you broke the seal while showing it to the prosecutor before trial, you may mention this.

Prosecutor:	Your Honor, may I approach the witness?
Judge:	Yes, you may.
Prosecutor:	Ms. Hernandez, I show you what has been marked for identification as Plaintiff's Exhibit # 13. Do you recognize it?
Witness:	Yes, I do.
Prosecutor:	Tell us what it is, please.
Witness:	(Examines item) It is the knife I found at the scene.
Prosecutor:	How do you know this is the knife you found at the scene?

Witness:	I put it in a bag, sealed it, and wrote my initials on the outside, along with the date that I did it.
Prosecutor:	Is it in the same condition as it was on the night you placed it into the bag?
Witness:	(Examines item again) Yes, it appears to be.
Prosecutor:	Is the seal intact?
Witness:	It is, but you and I examined the knife in your office last week so I opened the bag then. But after we looked at it, I put it back in the bag and resealed it. It has not been reopened since.
Prosecutor:	How do you know that?
Witness:	Because I sealed it with tape again and put my initials on it. The seal has not been broken.
Prosecutor:	Thank you. Your Honor, I offer Plaintiff's Exhibit # 13.
Defense counsel:	No objection, Your Honor.
Judge:	Exhibit # 13 is admitted.

Be certain, before you say so under oath, that the item is what you think it is. I have presided over cases where witnesses *assumed* exhibits were something other than what they really were. At best, it causes confusion to correct the mistake and reflects poorly on the witness who did not take the few seconds necessary to examine the exhibit before stating unequivocally that it is what the attorney and/or witness assumed it to be. At worst, an exhibit becomes part of the record when it should not have been admitted into evidence.

You may be able to tell at a glance what an exhibit is; nevertheless, it shows the jury that you are a careful person when you examine it before answering the lawyer's questions. You are under oath, after all. It reflects well on you, I think, for the jury to see that you take your role as a witness seriously.

Marking Documents

During cross-examination, you will often be asked to look at a document before questions are asked about it. Look it over closely from start to finish. If the attorney quotes a passage from the document, check to see whether it is being taken out of context. If the quote does not reflect the general tenor of the writing, say so.

You may be asked to put some mark, a circle, or initials, on a document, photograph or diagram. If you are at all uncertain about the location of a particular thing, give yourself some latitude by drawing a large circle or "X."

Identifying the Defendant

At some point in your testimony, you may be asked to identify the defendant. The examination typically goes like this.

Prosecutor:	Officer Klein, the person you arrested for theft on November 8, do you see him in this room?
Witness:	Yes, I do.
Prosecutor:	Would you point him out please?
Witness:	He's the man in the white shirt and blue tie, sitting at counsel table next to Attorney Abercrombie.
Prosecutor:	Let the record reflect the witness has identified the defendant.
Judge:	The record will so reflect.

When you make the identification, use your arm, hand, and finger to literally point out the defendant. Use a firm voice and identify the defendant without hesitation. You are certain of your identification. Let the judge and jury know it. It also makes for a better record if you use words to describe what the person is wearing. "He's wearing the white shirt with a brown tie at counsel table, sitting next to Attorney Renfrow," is better than, "He's the one sitting over there."

On a rare occasion, defense counsel may attempt to test a witness's ability to correctly identify the defendant by having the defendant sit in the audience next to other men similar in dress and appearance. If for any reason, you are unsure of your ability to identify the defendant, let the prosecutor know this immediately.

Requesting a Break

During a hearing or trial, the judge will ordinarily take a ten- to fifteen-minute recess every ninety minutes or so. There's no hard and fast rule but judges recognize it is uncomfortable for jurors and others to sit for long periods of time without a break. An old adage is followed by judges: "The brain can only absorb what the seat will endure."

It is possible you may be on the witness stand for a long time. If it has been more than an hour, and you need to use the bathroom or for some other reason need a break, ask for one. Simply turn to the judge and politely ask, "Your Honor, I'm really in need of a break. Will we be taking a recess soon?" The judge would likely address opposing counsel (you would not want to interrupt the flow of the prosecutor's examination unless absolutely necessary) and ask, "Mr. Compton, how long will it take to finish your questioning?" If the response is anything other than "I only have two or three more questions, Your Honor," the judge will likely take a recess immediately. Judges have bladders, too.

If the judge grants a recess, be sure you do not engage in *any* conversation with opposing counsel unless the prosecutor is present and has no objection. You are under no obligation to answer any questions put to you when you are not on the witness stand and testifying under oath. Attorneys can be cordial or overbearing. They may attempt to cajole you into "clarifying" some matter you just testified about or they may imply that you are required to talk to them. Do not fall for either ruse.

To draw from *Miranda*, "Anything you say can and will be used against you in a court of law." If you make the slightest admission of anything useful to defense counsel, rest assured it will be brought out when you return to the witness stand. Remember, you are not going to convince opposing counsel of anything and even if you did, the attorney is duty-bound to represent the client's interests. In other words, you have absolutely nothing to gain and you do have something to lose by engaging in conversation with opposing counsel.

The same goes for witnesses you know will be testifying on behalf of the defendant. Anything you say to them will likely be relayed to defense counsel. If it helps their case, believe me, it will be dragged out of you after the recess. My best advice: retire to a room where you can meet with the prosecutor or simply be away from other participants in the trial. Relax, unwind a bit, and think about the points you need to make when the questioning resumes.

Section Three: Make Effective Use of Visual Aids and Demonstrations

Lawyers are taught there are two ways of assuring the jury will remember a key point: repetition and multi-sensory input. Repetition is done by emphasizing the point in the lawyer's opening statement, again during examination of the witnesses, and yet again in closing argument. "Tell them what you're going to tell them, tell them again, and then tell them what you've told them," is the advice given lawyers by seasoned trial strategists. If you are going to rely only upon the spoken word to inform and persuade, repetition is often necessary.

Multi-sensory input usually means using visual and auditory methods to make a point. By and large, most evidence at trial is presented through oral testimony. This is only partially effective. Studies have shown jurors remember much more information if it is presented visually as well as orally.[7] A picture may truly be worth a thousand words.

Some jurors are auditory learners but they are in the minority. Most people are visual learners. The difficulty lies with the fact that any jury may include both auditory and visual learners. Some simply will not "get it" if facts are presented in only one manner. Any witness will greatly enhance a presentation by embodying both auditory and visual components. This takes careful thought and preparation.

Photographs

Photographs are probably used more often than any other visual aid, and for good reason. They tell the story more quickly and often more reliably than can be accomplished with verbal description. It is a rare case where photographs would not enhance the testimony of a witness.

For example, in a dispute over the worth of some personal property, such as an automobile, a photograph of it will give the jury or judge a much better idea of the item's condition than the words "dented" or "beat up." In a personal injury action, photographs of the injury or of the vehicles involved in the collision send a strong message that supplements and can even supplant testimony.

Photographs, like all exhibits, must be approved by the judge before a jury will be permitted to view them. Your attorney usually will have sought and gained this approval before trial. A judge can disallow photographs that are unduly "prejudicial" or irrelevant. Most judges won't keep out photographs on relevancy grounds but may exclude them if they are gruesome or gory. Nevertheless, in an appropriate case, even horrendous autopsy photos may be admitted.

Although photographs can be taken to the jury room for closer inspection, it is *always* a good idea to have them enlarged. Any photo developer can print the photos on a hard stock that allows them to be handled without fear of tearing or folding. I suggest all photos be eight inches by ten inches or larger. Another good presentation method is for the witness to use very large (18" x 24") photographs on the witness stand while jurors follow along by viewing smaller versions in photo albums prepared for each of them. An additional photo album should be given to the judge.

This latter point is important. Jurors need to see what you're talking about for the photo to have maximum impact. Sometimes attorneys make the mistake of admitting a photo into evidence, correctly asking for permission to present it to the jury for inspection, then continue with the questioning of the witness while the jurors are still passing the photo around the jury box. This is wrong! No one can listen attentively to testimony and examine a photograph at the same time. Additionally, jurors are distracted while the photograph is handed from one to the next. The correct procedure is for the attorney to ask the judge's permission to publish the photo to the jury, then *wait* until all have reviewed it before continuing with the examination.

If your lawyer is not adept and starts questioning you before every juror has seen the photograph you can politely ask, "Do you want me to wait until all of them have seen the photograph?" While your attorney may be a little embarrassed, jurors will secretly thank you.

When you are cross-examined, refer back to one of the photographs the jury saw earlier to make your point. "The Yield sign was located 100 feet from the place of impact. I believe you can see that on Exhibit #32." If the jurors still have their individual photo albums in their laps, many will instinctively open them to photo #32 as you are speaking. This is powerful reinforcement of a point you made earlier.

If used correctly, photographs can be your best support at trial. Use them to your advantage. Do not use more photographs than necessary as they lose their impact when jurors become overwhelmed with them. Moderation is good advice.

Demonstrations

How can you make a point visually? The means and methods are limited more by your imagination than by any rule of law. The judge has discretion to allow almost any kind of demonstration or to admit any exhibit for demonstration purposes. The test the judge uses to decide if the exhibit can be used in court is simple: Will the demonstration or exhibit make it easier for the jury to understand the witness's testimony? If the answer is "yes," and it almost invariably is, the demonstration will be allowed or the exhibit admitted.

You may want to brainstorm with your attorney and others about how to take advantage of this permissive rule. You can use charts, models, mannequins, photographs, maps, and anything else that can help you explain your testimony. You may be permitted to use a slide projector, blackboard, flip chart, or an ELMO visual presenter (a computerized overhead projector) to show something to the jury.

You may even be allowed to conduct an experiment in the courtroom. During one murder trial, a forensic chemist testified about his examination of the murder scene. A young man had been bludgeoned to death while he slept on the defendant's bed. The body was gone when the chemist arrived on the scene and the walls looked clean but were not.

"I figured the suspect probably wiped the wall down," the chemist told the jury. "I had a chemical reagent with me that would detect the presence of blood," he continued. "So I sprayed it on that part of the wall where I thought there might be some blood. I then used a fluoroscope to illuminate the area. The presence of blood shows up green under the fluoroscope," he explained.

"Would it assist the jury to understand your testimony if you could demonstrate here in court what you did on the night you examined the scene?" I asked. "Yes, it would," the chemist answered. Over defense counsel's objection, the judge allowed us to conduct the experiment.

The chemist took a piece of wallpaper identical to that found at the scene, put a few drops of blood on it, wiped the blood off with a paper towel, then sprayed the chemical reagent on the stained area. The lights in the courtroom were dimmed. The chemist turned on his fluoroscope and shown it on the stained area. It was a highly dramatic moment in the trial. And then, nothing! The blood didn't show at all. The experiment was a complete flop.

There is a lesson here. Never, I repeat, never conduct an experiment in court without first practicing it outside the courtroom. If you are asked by opposing counsel to participate in a demonstration, be wary. Often, the defense will want you to step down off the stand and show the jury how an event occurred. If you are asked to assume the role of someone other than yourself, be sure to point out differences in your height and weight, strength, or other applicable factors as you are engaged in the demonstration. "Of course, I am a lot taller and heavier than your client, Mr. Vinje."

If defense counsel has you demonstrate things in a manner that differs from the actual event, be sure to point it out. Nothing in the rules says you have to remain quiet during a demonstration. If opposing counsel gets exasperated with you, she or he may tell you not to speak unless questioned. If that happens, look to the judge and say, "I'll do whatever you require me to do, Your Honor." Then follow those instructions. Remember, the attorney does not have authority to control the courtroom or anything that happens inside; the judge does.

Charts

There are several things to keep in mind when using charts. Most trial lawyers will tell you that an exhibit which appears to have been prepared by a professional will be more persuasive than something that looks homemade. I think it depends on the exhibit. Sometimes a folksy approach is as effective as a more polished one. Consult with your attorney about this. In trial law, there are few absolutes.

But here is one of them. Make sure the chart and all printing on it are large enough to be seen at a distance of fifteen to twenty feet. Another good reason to visit the courtroom where the trial will be held is to measure the distance from the chair in the top row of the jury box to the place where you will be using the exhibit. Ask someone to sit in that juror's chair and give you feedback on the visibility of the exhibit. If they can't see it, you've wasted a great deal of time and energy preparing it for use at trial.

Unlike photographs, charts generally are not admitted as evidence. When jurors retire to deliberate, they can take with them the photographs and any other items that have been received into evidence. Since charts are used for "demonstrative purposes" only, to demonstrate a point, they are not taken into the jury room at the end of the trial. This is yet another reason why charts have to be made in such a way that they can be easily viewed.

Generally speaking, the fewer words printed on a chart or exhibit, the better. Use the exhibit to explain concepts or ideas. Don't try to include the entire exposition on the exhibit. The exhibit enhances your testimony; it is not a substitute for it.

As is true with photographs, you can overdo it with too many charts. If each chart contains several complex components, jurors may inwardly groan when you place Chart #4 on the easel. If your testimony is so difficult to understand that you need several charts to explain it, your case is probably in trouble with a jury and even with some judges. Lawyers are often advised at trial seminars to remember the KISS principle: Keep It Simple, Stupid. The easier it is for the jury to understand a subject, the greater the likelihood of prevailing on that issue.

The lesson for witnesses is to simplify as much as possible when testifying about difficult or complex matters. Gear your presentation so it will be readily understood by jurors with an eighth grade education and you will succeed more times than not.

When presenting anything on a chart, be sure of two things. First, talk to the jury, not to the chart. Sometimes it is helpful to use a pointer instead of your hand or finger to identify something on the chart. Locate it, then turn to your audience, the jury, and say what you have to say. Second, stand to the side of the chart, not anywhere that blocks any juror's view of the chart. This is another good reason to use a pointer. You would be surprised at the number of witnesses who violate one or both of these rules. That beautiful chart you labored so hard to prepare is of little value if all of the jurors cannot see it or cannot hear what you have to say about it.

The best advice for using charts effectively is to practice. If you have a patient companion with you on the day you visit the courtroom in advance of trial, ask him or her to listen to your presentation. Then seek a critique, not so much on the substance of your discourse, but on your delivery and the visibility of the chart.

The Flip Chart or Blackboard

Most courtrooms are equipped with a flip chart or blackboard, something a witness can write or draw on. Almost all of us grew up with blackboards in school but many have never used a flip chart. The flip chart is simply a large tablet of white paper mounted on an easel. You draw on a sheet, flip it over the top of the easel, or tear it off, then write on another.

More often than not, if you are asked to draw something, it will be at the request of opposing counsel. Your attorney would typically prefer that you use a prepared chart or document. Drawing on blackboards or flip charts is usually done for demonstrative purposes. Therefore, the written products are typically not taken into the jury room when the jurors deliberate.

This makes the presentation in the courtroom all the more important. What was said earlier with regard to charts applies to blackboards and flip charts. Make sure the audience hears what you are saying as you draw. Do not stand in the way of the drawing as you explain what it depicts.

Other things to keep in mind are geographical directions, size, and descriptions for the record. By geographical directions, I am referring to those you find on a map: north, south, east, and west. All maps in the United States have the direction north on the top of the document; west is always on the left; east on the right; and the bottom of the document is south. Be sure your drawing complies with these standards; anything else may be confusing to jurors (sometimes opposing counsel purposely contributes to the confusion).

Size is important in that whatever you draw must be legible from fifteen to twenty feet away. That means you have to depict things larger than may seem natural to you. If you print the names of buildings or streets, or if you label vehicles at the scene of a collision, be sure to do so in large letters. Alternatively, you may use one large letter, "D" for example, to denote the Defendant's car. Just be sure to explain this to the jury as you are writing.

Draw in proportion. If you are asked to draw the intersection where two vehicles collided, don't make a car larger than the street on which it traveled. Think ahead. How will you respond if asked to draw the rooms in a house or a stretch of highway, assuming those subjects are likely to be covered during your examination?

The "record" refers to the transcript that will be reviewed by a higher court if there is an appeal from the jury's verdict. With regard to flip charts and blackboards, bear in mind that the appellate court will not have the benefit of seeing what you draw. The record will include only your words. Do not use words like "here" and "there" when describing something in court, e.g., "The red car was over here." Instead, say "I'm making an 'X' on the left side of the diagram to show where the red car was located in the ditch on the west side of the road."

If you are drawing a map of the house where you executed a search warrant and describing where you found key evidence, the record must accurately reflect what happened. Imagine the unfortunate appellate justices who have to figure out where items were located from this record: "We went to the front door, here. Then we went inside and over here to the living room. Then we went in here and found the powdery substance. Under here, we found the baggie with marijuana in it. In the bedroom, over here, we found the scale and owe sheets."

Here, again, practice makes perfect. If you have any inkling that you will be called upon to draw the scene and describe an event, get yourself to a courtroom with a friend and try it out before the trial. Ask your audience to pay careful attention to the words you use in describing what happened. Then modify your approach as needed.

Other Exhibits

Jurors like to see and feel things that are new to them. While a bong or a weigh scale may be old hat to you, it will enliven your testimony if you can use it for a little show and tell. This not only captivates your audience, but it gives you a golden opportunity to demonstrate your knowledge and expertise.

You may use anything which makes your testimony more easily understood so do some brainstorming and you will undoubtedly come up with several items that could be used to enhance your testimony. And you are not limited to one item but may use several if you want to, assuming the judge goes along. Most will.

If you are keeping the jury interested in your presentation, the judge will most likely be interested as well. Judges, more than anyone else, are easily bored. They've heard most everything before so whatever you can do to liven things up will probably be appreciated so long as you don't take an inordinate amount of time to conduct your demonstration.

Again, the key is to practice with the object so that your presentation to the jury will go smoothly. If you properly use the exhibit, you can enhance your credibility in the eyes of the jury.

Section Four: Some Dos and Don'ts at Trial

Tip #1: Do not bring a cell phone into the courtroom

Often, as you pass through a metal detector on your way into a courthouse, you will be cautioned about cell phone usage. Many courtrooms have signs posted outside them directing people to turn off all cell phones or place them on vibrate. Despite the warnings, some people receive phone calls or texts while they are in a courtroom. Judges look upon such conduct with great disfavor.

Recently, a judge heard a ringtone on someone's cell phone during arraignment of a defendant. "All right," said the judge, "whose phone is that?" Sheepishly, one of the attorneys at counsel table admitted it was his. "I'm terribly sorry, Your Honor. I thought I had turned it off but I must have forgotten. It won't happen again."

"You, sir, are in contempt," the judge said. "Bailiff, take this man to jail." The attorney spent the better part of the day in jail before the judge let him out. Do not let this happen to you. Leave your cell phone at home or in your vehicle when you have to testify.

Tip #2: Do prepare answers to anticipated "stock" questions

Good prosecutors will want to enhance your credibility with the jury or judge by having you tell something about yourself with which the listener can identify. The questioning may go like this:

Prosecutor:	Please introduce yourself to the jury.
Witness:	My name is Peter Carvell.
Prosecutor:	Would you tell us a little about yourself?
Witness:	I'm a sergeant with the Bismarck Police Department. I'm married and we have two grown children. Both my wife and I grew up in North Dakota and we've lived here all our lives. I attended the University of North Dakota in Grand Forks where I earned my bachelor's degree in Criminal Justice. In my spare time, I like to officiate softball games and do some fishing.

There are no blanket rules applicable to this kind of question. Most judges allow it on the basis that it helps the jury determine credibility. Rarely, an impatient judge may jump in and stop the witness from answering. Nevertheless, it helps to be prepared to answer this stock question.

As for content, every tidbit of information may resonate with one or more jurors so it does not hurt to add some detail to your narrative. The fact that you are married will be a plus in the minds of most married folks. Parents identify with other parents. Someone on the jury may be an avid softball player or angler. If you are unsure whether or not to include a particular piece of the biographical sketch, ask your attorney for advice.

Tip #3: Do make sure you understand the question

Attorneys have bad days, just like everyone else. Especially when the attorney is asking questions based on previous testimony and without adequate preparation, questions can become convoluted. To illustrate, this is an excerpt from an actual trial:

Defense counsel:	When he went, had you gone and had she, if she wanted to and were able, for the time being excluding all the restraints on her not to go, gone also, would he have brought you, meaning you and she, with him to the station?
Prosecutor:	Objection. That question should be taken out and shot.

Sometimes the question refers to earlier testimony but this is clear only in the questioner's mind, e.g., "You're saying then, that because they did this, you had to do it, too?" The judge does not expect that you will be able to adequately answer jumbled questions and the judge wants the matter to be clear for the record. If your attorney objects to the form of the question, the judge will likely sustain the objection and ask the interrogator to rephrase. If there is no objection, it is advisable to ask for clarification. "I don't think I understand what you are asking me." Be polite. Don't impugn the skills of the examining attorney, but simply evoke an attitude of wanting to be helpful. "Could you please rephrase that question so that I can better understand it?"

Attorneys will sometimes ask compound questions. A compound question is one which actually contains two questions. Some attorneys ask them deliberately to confuse the witness or in an attempt to get a concession, but most are simply less careful with their language than they ought to be.

Here is an example: "You have a four-year-old daughter who is hyperactive, don't you?" A proper response might be: "Yes, I have a four-year-old daughter, but I would not agree that she is hyperactive."

Another example is: "What color was the traffic light and how fast were the two cars going when they got to the intersection?" A good response is, "Could you rephrase that please?" or "I'm sorry, counsel, which part of your question do you want me to answer first?"

Tip #4: Do not use profanity

It should go without saying that you should not use profanity while in the courtroom. It's not that the judge and most, if not all, of the jurors haven't done their share of swearing. But there is a strong taboo against conduct that reduces the dignity afforded court proceedings. The judge, by rule, has the power to punish transgressors on the spot. An attorney who swears in court will probably be fined; the same is true for the client.

A witness who swears on the stand may get by with only an admonition from the judge if the apology follows the outburst before the judge has to respond. "Oops, sorry, Your Honor, that slipped; it won't happen again." But an unrepentant witness is begging for a dressing down by the judge, at a minimum. This can't help but diminish the witness's credibility in the eyes of the jury.

Like any other rule, there are exceptions. When a witness is quoting the exact language used by another, it is permissible to swear. If this should arise during your testimony, I suggest you first turn to the judge and seek permission to use the salty language.

Prosecutor:	What did Mr. Martin say when you asked him for his license and registration?
Officer:	Your Honor, should I use the exact words he used?
Judge:	Yes, you may.
Officer:	He said, "You sons of bitches have nuthin' better to do than pick on law-abiding citizens. I'm getting sick of this shit."

These questions will usually arise on direct examination and you will most likely know ahead of time that the question is coming. So prepare your answer accordingly.

Another time you may use profanity is on cross-examination when you are quoting language you used at an earlier time. Here it is important to be candid. If you used profanity, admit it. If you don't admit it, opposing counsel will exaggerate the issue.

Opposing counsel:	After you rear-ended my client, and she got out of her car, what was the first thing you said to her?
Witness:	I said something like, you shouldn't have stopped so fast. I didn't have a chance to stop.
Opposing counsel:	That's not what you really said, is it?
Witness:	Something like that; maybe not those exact words.
Opposing counsel:	Tell us what you really said.
Witness:	I'm not sure I remember the exact words.
Opposing counsel:	You used some profanity, didn't you?
Witness:	I may have.
Opposing counsel:	Come on, now, sir, you called her a "dumb bitch," didn't you?
Witness:	I could have.
Opposing counsel:	You screamed at her, "You dumb bitch, you made me hit you," didn't you?
Witness:	I probably did.
Opposing counsel:	Were you having trouble controlling your temper that day?
Witness:	Not really, no.
Opposing counsel:	So that's how you respond to situations where something angers you?
Witness:	No.
Opposing counsel:	Was something else bothering you when you were driving down the street just before the crash?
Witness:	No.

Opposing counsel can drag this out for quite a while, all of which could have been avoided by answering like this:

Opposing counsel:	After you rear-ended my client, and she got out of her car, what was the first thing you said to her?
Witness:	Your Honor, I apologize for using this language in your courtroom. I said, "You dumb bitch, you made me hit you." Ms. Jones [look at her], I'm sorry for swearing at you.

If you apologized to Ms. Jones before court, make that clear. "Ms. Jones [look at her], I again apologize to you for my conduct. I'm sorry." Not only have you done the right thing by apologizing, now you have disarmed the opposition. Please note that when you recite the swear words, you can give the language the emphasis you desire. Know that when opposing counsel quotes you, the inflection and tone will be harsher. The lesson is to control that which you can while on the witness stand.

Tip #5: Do not argue

There will be times when opposing counsel asks questions which seem totally unrelated to the issues before the court. The temptation is to tell opposing counsel to "get with the program" and redirect attention to the matters of importance. I've heard witnesses, in response to cross-examination, say "That's irrelevant!"

What follows typically is a request from opposing counsel for the judge to order the witness to answer the question. That is, if the judge hasn't jumped in first and instructed the witness, "I decide what's relevant in here. That's what I get paid to do. Answer the question!" In either case, the witness's attempt to argue with opposing counsel backfires.

It requires a degree of faith, but you have to rely on your attorney to make proper and timely objections to irrelevant or otherwise hostile questions. Surprisingly to many people, the questions are relevant and a judge will allow them even if an objection is raised. For example, questions that challenge a witness's bias or perception are perfectly proper though they don't relate to the specific facts of the case.

Jurors are human. If they see that opposing counsel is "beating up" a witness for no apparent reason, they may hold it against that attorney. Even if they don't, your attorney may make the point in closing argument that, "The opposition's case is so weak they spent their time questioning our witnesses about entirely irrelevant matters. They did not, because they could not, challenge the strengths of our case. That is why they tried to distract you with these details unrelated to the case." This may be your attorney's strategy, to make the point during closing argument, rather than raise an objection during your testimony. So don't get disgusted if your attorney does not object to questions which seem irrelevant. Roll with it.

Tip #6: Do speak in your own words

It is important that you use your own words when testifying. If you try to memorize what someone else has written for you, your nonverbal language will give you away. Using a more erudite vocabulary in an effort to impress jurors is bound to backfire, particularly if opposing counsel is adept at exposing it.

This is not to say that you should "dumb down" your language. Experts often use terminology with which the average lay person is unfamiliar. This does not mean the expert should avoid using a technical term but only that the term should be defined or explained immediately after it is used.

Prosecutor:	Officer, did anything unusual happen around 10:30 that night?
Officer:	We received a report of a 10-10, that is a fight in progress, at Bud's Pub.

Although most people in the courtroom will know that an APB is an "all points bulletin," if one or two jurors do not understand the abbreviation, some important testimony may be lost. As a general rule, avoid jargon and abbreviations. You would be surprised at the number of people who have no idea what those terms or letters represent.

Tip #7: Do not interrupt the questioner

You should have been briefed in advance of trial about the questions that will be asked of you on direct examination. The judge or jury may expect such preparation to have occurred but it is still not a good practice to be overt about it. In other words, try not to give the jury the impression that this is simply a script that you and your attorney are following.

If you interrupt your attorney, it will usually happen because you have anticipated the question and are anxious to make your response. Strictly speaking, this violates court procedures though it is unlikely anyone will object. But to interrupt is discourteous and it implies your answer has been overly rehearsed. So never interrupt your attorney.

Don't interrupt opposing counsel either. When you interrupt opposing counsel, it is usually because you disagree with the point being made through the question. When you answer before the full question is stated, opposing counsel may object or tell you, "Please let me finish my question before you respond." This makes you look argumentative as well as impolite. If you repeatedly interrupt, you may draw an admonition from the judge, something you always want to avoid.

There is a more important reason for not interrupting questions from opposing counsel. It is to allow your attorney time to raise an objection to the question. Far more often than you might expect, questions will be asked by attorneys which violate one of a host of legal rules. The Rules of Evidence guide all trials, whether before a judge or jury. When opposing counsel asks a question in violation of one of the rules, your attorney may, but is not required to, object to the question.

Timing is crucial! If you answer the question before your attorney objects, the damage cannot be undone. In most cases, your attorney will not bother to object because the judge may rule against your attorney or because a favorable ruling does not "unring" the bell.

If you have blurted out your answer and the judge sustains your attorney's objection, the judge will say something to the effect of

"Members of the jury, you will disregard the answer to that last question." This doesn't help your case much and may actually reinforce the testimony which should not have been heard by the jury in the first place. Wait for opposing counsel to finish every question, pause long enough for your attorney to object, then, if there is no objection, answer the question.

Tip #8: Do listen to the objections

You are not a lawyer and no one expects you to be one on the witness stand. No one thinks you should have a command of the Rules of Evidence when you formulate your answers to questions from the attorneys. Nevertheless, it may be helpful for you to know something about the most common objections made during the course of any trial: hearsay and lack of foundation.

Hearsay

Perhaps the most frequent objection in any trial is "hearsay," as in "Objection, Your Honor, the question calls for hearsay." Hearsay statements are out-of-court statements made by persons which are introduced for the purpose of proving the truth of the matter asserted in the statement. Some examples:

> "My daughter Linda said that Boyd gave her the black eye."
>
> "My son told me he was roughed up at school by the Johnson boy."

There can even be hearsay upon hearsay, or "double hearsay," e.g., "The neighbor told my husband who told me that it was her dog that bit the child."

If these statements are offered to prove the truth of the matters asserted (that Boyd hit Linda, that a son was roughed up by the Johnson boy, or that the neighbor's dog bit a child), they are hearsay. Generally speaking, hearsay is inadmissible in court. The reason for the hearsay rule goes to the very heart of our adversarial system of justice.

It is assumed that if both sides are able to present their case to the trier-of-fact, the truth will be brought out. The assumption rests on the guarantee of cross-examination. The theory is that truth will best be revealed if all witnesses are subject to close questioning by the opposition. The process of cross-examination should reveal weaknesses, gaps, and inconsistencies in the testimony.

When hearsay is accepted into evidence, the party against whom the testimony is offered is cheated the opportunity of cross-examination. Without Linda on the witness stand, the opposing party cannot determine why she told her mother that Boyd struck her.

Please note I said "generally speaking, hearsay is inadmissible." There are more than twenty well-recognized exceptions to that general rule barring admissibility. The most common is the exception for statements made by an opposing party. If Boyd told Linda he was going to keep punching her until she started listening to him, his statement could be brought out at trial through Linda's testimony because it is an admission by an opposing party.

But what is important for you to know is that when opposing counsel objects to a question from the prosecutor on the basis of hearsay, the objection will require the judge to mentally review the exceptions to the general rule and decide whether or not you can answer. Wait for the ruling before answering. If the judge sustains (upholds) the objection made by opposing counsel, your attorney will rephrase the question or move to another topic.

Frequently, the question may not ask for hearsay but the witness's response will include it nonetheless. For example:

Prosecutor:	"Do you know how Linda got her black eye?"
Witness:	"Well, she told me that Boyd hit her with his fist."

Defense counsel will properly object that the response includes hearsay and should be stricken from the record. Most likely, the judge will do just that.

A correct response to the question would be "No," or "I only know what Linda told me." Attorneys seek to avoid objectionable questions so listen carefully to the exact words used. Avoid hearsay unless you've discussed the matter with your attorney. By understanding the rationale behind this common objection, your responses are less likely to be stricken from the record.

Lack of Foundation

Another frequent objection is that a question "lacks foundation." As with other objections, if the judge agrees, you will not be allowed to answer the question even though you clearly know the answer!

Assume you were the arresting officer who charged Mr. Schmidt with driving under the influence of intoxicating beverages. The prosecutor has asked you questions about your name, occupation, training, and general law enforcement experience. These questions follow:

Prosecutor:	Were you on duty around 1:30 a.m., Saturday, August 5?
Officer:	Yes, I was.
Prosecutor:	Did you arrest anyone for DWI at about that time?
Officer:	Yes, I did. I arrested Mr. Schmidt.
Prosecutor:	Do you have an opinion as to whether or not Mr. Schmidt was under the influence of intoxicating liquor that night?
Defense counsel:	Objection! Lack of foundation.
Judge:	Sustained.

The objection was sustained because the prosecutor has not laid the necessary groundwork, the foundation, for asking you the ultimate question. To lay the groundwork, the prosecutor would have to ask several questions about Mr. Schmidt's conduct, both while driving, and while performing field sobriety tests. In addition, the prosecutor would want to question you specifically about your experience with impaired drivers. Once that is done, you may be allowed to give your opinion about Mr. Schmidt's degree of impairment.

The important thing for you to know when opposing counsel objects to a "lack of foundation," is that there is groundwork that needs to be completed before you can answer the question. With this knowledge, you will have a better understanding of where the attorney is going with the next series of questions.

Tip #9: Do not converse with opposing counsel

> "Never say anything on the phone that you wouldn't want your mother to hear at your trial." (Advice to women she employed in her escort service) — Sydney Biddle Barrows, *Mayflower Madam*

After you have testified, especially in cases where your testimony was lengthy, the judge may call a recess. Many attorneys for the opposition use this opportunity to obtain information from the witness who has just left the stand. "So what?" you think to yourself, "I'm done testifying. There can't be any harm in talking to the opposition now." If you believe this, you may be in for a rude awakening.

The reasons for steering clear of opposing counsel are manifold. First, whether you want to or not, you may be recalled to testify by either side in the case. Your attorney may want you to clarify some testimony or counteract something another witness said. Once you resume the stand, you are subject to cross-examination. Although the cross-examining attorney is supposed to confine the questions to the subject matter just covered by your attorney, judges are sometimes very lenient in allowing cross-examination on tangential matters.

If opposing counsel believes you have information valuable to her client which was not brought out when you were last on the witness stand, the attorney can call you as her witness. Some seemingly small detail you gave her in the hallway may be magnified in the courtroom and turn the whole case around. If you inadvertently give defense counsel some valuable information, believe me, it will be used to hurt the prosecution's case.

Even if defense counsel doesn't get any information of value to the defendant from you, the very fact that you are seen having the conversation may be helpful to the defendant. Let me explain. If any juror sees you and defense counsel conversing, maybe laughing at a joke together, but, in any event, looking like chums, that juror may assume you don't think the prosecution's case is a serious one. Why else would you so readily "consort with the enemy"? While you know this is not reality, after all, you are not supposed to be anyone's enemy, the juror does not. My advice: when approached by defense counsel, politely, but firmly, say that you are not free to discuss the case unless the prosecutor is present.

Attorneys can be very cordial and charming; they may only want to take a moment of your time to "clarify" something. Stick to your guns no matter how persuasive or threatening opposing counsel becomes. "You can talk to me now, or I can subpoena you and make you return to court," the defense attorney may warn. Your response should be, "Do whatever you think you must." Then walk away.

Apply this same caution to surrogates of opposing counsel. It may be a legal assistant or a witness sympathetic to the opposition who attempts to get information from you. Regardless of the source, do not engage in conversation about anything related to the case unless your attorney has approved it in advance.

This is good advice even after the jury retires to deliberate on a verdict. There is always the possibility of a mistrial or a new trial following an appeal. In other words, don't assume the case is over simply because both sides have rested their case.

Section Five: How to Be Verbally Persuasive on the Witness Stand

Tip #1: Tell the truth

"A liar needs a good memory."—Quintilian

There are many reasons to always tell the truth on the witness stand. Not the least of these is the oath you take. Whether you "swear to tell the truth, the whole truth, and nothing but the truth so help you God," or "affirm under the penalties of perjury to tell the truth," you are legally bound to answer questions without prevarication. If you lie, you can be charged with perjury, a felony in most states.

In reality, very few people are charged with perjury. Defendants in criminal cases rarely take the witness stand. That is so because the attorneys who represent them are under an ethical obligation not to present testimony believed to be false. In other words, if the client tells the lawyer that he intends to testify falsely, the lawyer cannot call the client to the stand without violating the Code of Professional Responsibility, the ethical rules governing lawyers' conduct.

Even when defendants do testify and a jury disbelieves them, as shown by a guilty verdict, it is an extremely rare case where the prosecutor then pursues perjury charges against them. The reasons are pragmatic. First, to prove perjury there must be evidence of a false statement under oath. This is not as simple to prove as one might think. If a witness's statement is in any way based on perception or opinion, it is almost impossible to prove intentional lying.

Second, an element of the crime of perjury is materiality. It is not enough to prove a misstatement under oath; the misstatement must relate to an issue which is "material" to the general matter testified about. For example, in a prosecution for driving under the influence, if the defendant testified he only had two beers when he consumed ten, that is a material matter and the defendant could be charged with perjury. But if the defendant testified he arrived at the bar at 8:30 p.m. knowing that he had actually arrived there at 6:30 p.m., the false testimony would likely be deemed immaterial to the offense of driving under the influence.

This is not to suggest you should entertain the thought of being less than honest about matters which do not go to the heart of the case before the jury. You're much better off being completely candid, even when it hurts.

In virtually every case which goes to trial, there are weaknesses on both sides. The adversary system is designed to reveal these weaknesses to the trier-of-fact, the judge or jury. Just as there are weaknesses in each side of the case, there are usually weaknesses in the testimony of each witness. There often are facts known by each witness which bolster the other side's case.

The temptation is to cover them up, or worse, lie about them. This is not a good strategy because any competent attorney may know about them in advance of trial and bring them out, one way or another. An attempt to hide unfavorable evidence usually backfires. Opposing counsel will not only reveal the facts sought to be hidden, but go to great lengths to discredit the witness who has attempted to keep them from coming to light. Although this is not an internally consistent argument, time and again I've seen defense attorneys argue that a jury should believe the "favorable" testimony from a police officer but should completely disregard the rest of the officer's testimony because of an attempted cover up.

Rational jurors do not expect cases to be airtight. They know nothing is all black or white. They expect certain inconsistencies and contradictions. But they also expect complete honesty from every law enforcement officer. They expect you to admit the weaknesses in the case if you have personal knowledge of them. When you do, you actually enhance your credibility with jurors and the judge.

Good attorneys use testimonial inconsistencies to their advantage. The attorney for one side argues the inconsistencies show the witness is untrustworthy in all respects. Opposing counsel argues that the jury should believe a witness because he or she admitted certain unfavorable facts.

The lab scientist who admitted misplacing a piece of evidence, the social worker who admitted a bias toward a particularly obnoxious family member, or the police officer who frankly admitted failure to give an accused the Miranda warnings: all come across as more credible because they freely admitted their error.

Defensiveness has just the opposite effect and gives opposing counsel the red herring needed to divert attention from a client's guilt or negligence. A case that was a hopeless loser for the defendant takes on new life; now, the case is all about the "prosecution's lying witness." Don't let it happen to you. Tell the truth, always.

For example, if you are the officer who cited a motorist with speeding, the trial may take place weeks or months after the event. Meanwhile, you've issued dozens of other citations. At trial, the defense asks: "Did you offer to show Mr. Jennings the locked-in speed on your radar machine?" or "Didn't Mr. Jennings tell you he had his cruise control set under the speed limit?" If you do not remember the case well enough to say, for sure, what happened, readily admit it.

You are permitted to say, "I don't have a specific recollection of offering Mr. Jennings the opportunity to look at the locked-in speed but that is my usual operating procedure." Under Rule 406, Federal Rules of Evidence, and in most states, your habit or custom will probably be admitted as evidence.

Whatever the temptation to bend the truth, resist it. It is not worth your reputation or your career to convict someone on false evidence. Many defendants are recidivists and will be back in court on other charges soon. There will be another day.

Tip #2: Attitude counts

> "A joke, even if it be a lame one, is nowhere so keenly relished or quickly applauded as in a murder trial." — Mark Twain [Samuel Langhorne Clemens]

Because trials are often emotionally charged events, tensions run high in the courtroom. To ease the tension, sometimes injecting a clever comment or joke seems appropriate. I suggest you refrain from it.

The problem with humor is that not everyone has a sense of one; a corollary is that we all have different ideas about what is funny and what is not. With a jury, the odds are that someone on the jury will think your attempt at humor is about as funny as a trip to the mortuary. You may not lose points with every juror for being quick-witted but there is enough of a probability that you will offend one juror for you to exercise restraint.

Some defense counsel in criminal cases want to inject humor in the case. Their rationale may be that it will be easier for the jury to acquit the defendant if jurors believe the case isn't very serious. For that reason, prosecutors seldom want humor to creep into the courtroom during trial. By engaging in humor, you may be playing into the hands of the defendant.

One final reason not to use humor is that it seldom translates well in print. Remember that an appellate court, or your boss, reviewing a transcript of the trial will not have the benefit of everything seen and heard in the courtroom. They will have only the cold, hard record. The comical look on someone's face, or the tone of the words spoken may make something downright hilarious in court but fail to come across as even slightly humorous on paper.

Always display good manners. Jurors love someone who can maintain composure while undergoing tough cross-examination. They've watched enough television and movies to know that attorneys are given plenty of latitude when cross-examining a witness. Many of them expect the cross-examiner to be ruthless and crass because that's what they've been exposed to in the media.

The truth is, far too many cross-examiners are not as well prepared as the actors who play the roles on the screen. Their questions tend to be undramatic. Cross-examination, in the real world, often tends to be overly long and not particularly productive.

The best cross-examiners are concise and unemotional. They cut and run, often scoring points that do not become obvious until later in the trial. One of the best trial lawyers, Irving Younger, taught attorneys to never attempt to make more than three points during cross-examination. "Get in, slice and dice, and get out." Nevertheless, there is at least a decent chance that you will run across an attorney who confuses rudeness with good lawyering. How do you deal with that attorney?

Although you may have to grit your teeth, the answer is to remain professional and low key at all times. Respond to sarcasm without a tinge of it in your voice. Respond to phony anger with tranquility. I suggest using "Sir" or "Ma'am" in your answers. "No sir, I would have to disagree with that." "Yes, ma'am, that is how I conducted the test."

Jurors don't like hotheads, and they simply don't trust people who lose control on the witness stand unless it is a victim of a crime being badgered mercilessly by a defense counsel. And for some reason, jurors seldom hold it against the repugnant attorney who engages in rude behavior. The Canons of Ethics for attorneys require them to "zealously represent" their client. Perhaps jurors know, at some deep level, that attorneys are required to fight hard and even get "dirty," so jurors forgive them their excesses. "He's just doing his job," they may conclude.

In any event, it's important for you to know that jurors probably won't penalize, with their verdict, the obnoxious attorney. But the same is not true for you as a witness. It's a double standard and hardly a fair one, but it is reality.

Tip #3: Choose your words carefully

> "The difference between the right word and the *almost* right word is the difference between lightning and the lightning bug." —Mark Twain [Samuel Langhorne Clemens]

Psychologists demonstrated that the words we use when we question others affect responses. Test subjects in a virtual environment witnessed a car collision. They were then asked a series of questions. One group of test subjects was asked, "How far from the street were you when you saw the red car?" Another group of test subjects was asked, "How close to the street were you when you saw the red car?" Those who answered the first question gave an approximation significantly longer in distance than those who answered the second question.

In another experiment, test subjects were asked to estimate the height of an individual seen in a movie. Half of the subjects were asked, "How tall was the man?" The other half were asked, "How short was the man?" The averaged results showed the "tall" man subjects estimated a height ten inches taller than the "short" man subjects.[8] Savvy attorneys are aware of this and may incorporate the appropriate term, from their perspective, in their question to you. Listen for it.

Seasoned trial attorneys also know that jurors look at the attorney and client as one entity. To take advantage of this concept, criminal defense attorneys will cozy up to their client in public to give jurors the impression that they are friends. The implicit argument is, "Look, folks, this guy can't be too bad because I'm a college-educated professional and he's a buddy of mine."

Defense attorneys will often personalize the client by calling him "Bob" rather than "Mr. Fleischer." Conversely, the same attorney will attempt to depersonalize others by referring to them as "the Plaintiff," "the Petitioner," "the alleged victim," or "the Respondent." The attorney might refer to an opponent by their profession, e.g., "the chiropractor," or "the accountant." This is an attempt to create a greater psychological distance between the jury and the person so described.

You can influence jurors' perception through your choice of language. Unless you are using an exhibit, your best means of conveying a concept or recollection to the jury is choosing your vocabulary carefully. Different words permit the listener to draw subtle distinctions. It is one thing to say a drunk "walked" to the detention center. But you can use more descriptive verbs. An inebriated person may "weave," "shuffle," "stumble," "lurch," or "creep."

If you want to emphasize the seriousness of an injury you may want to describe a wound as a "laceration" rather than a "cut," a "contusion" rather than a "bruise." Do you refer to the car crash as an "accident" or a "collision"? "Collision" implies fault or is at least neutral on causation; "accident" implies the incident could not have been prevented. The word you choose may influence the listener and the choice is entirely yours. You can paint the picture the way you like while not straying from the truth. A thesaurus can be a most useful tool for the well-prepared witness.

Tip #4: Use powerful language

Just as you can convey confidence and professionalism through your nonverbal language, you can enhance your credibility through the use of powerful language. To be powerful, the words you use must not be ambiguous and your phraseology should be positive.

The opposite of powerful language is weak or unconvincing language. Examples of weak language include any sentence which begins: "It seems like...," or "I believe ..." A witness who describes a scene by testifying it is "kind of like" signals to the jury some confusion exists in the witness's mind about the event. Instead, say it is what it is. When you are stating an opinion, you need not preface it with, "In my opinion, ..." The jury knows it is your opinion. Be positive. Be clear. You will persuade.

Tip #5: Use examples, stories and analogies

> "You never truly understand a thing until you can explain it to your grandmother."—Albert Einstein

Psychologists tell us people remember analogies, stories, and examples better than any other testimony. This is especially true when complicated matters are explained to persons who have little or no background in the subject area.

In a murder case where the defendant pled not guilty by reason of insanity, a psychiatrist was called upon to testify about the defendant's mental health. The defense had made quite a production out of showing the defendant suffered a concussion on the night of the murder. The psychiatrist explained to the jury that simply because the defendant suffered a concussion did not mean that he was more prone to mental illness or defect than anyone else.

The jury was comprised of older-than-average citizens and the psychiatrist used an apt analogy. "Experiencing a concussion," he said, "was like the switchboard operator in an old-time telephone office. All of the phone wires are jerked out of their sockets and all activity stops. But the phone equipment is not really damaged. Plug the wires back in and the connections are fine. People can talk to one another again. The brain operates in the same way. The concussion knocked out all the connections for a while but when the patient regains consciousness, most likely there is no long-term damage. The individual can be back to normal almost immediately."

Examples and analogies work best when they arise from our shared experiences. Our culture is changing, some say dramatically, in that those shared experiences are now more often associated with the visual media. References to literary characters or novels may draw blank stares from many younger jurors. Instead, television sitcom characters or movie roles may be better known.

Since you will usually not know the makeup of the jury until the day you testify, it helps to give this matter some forethought. How will you explain something to the grandmother in the second row while also clarifying it for the nineteen-year-old in the front row? What example can you use that will be equally clear to both? With preparation, you will find something that works.

Tip #6: Pay attention to cadence and inflection

This advice is targeted at that cadre of witnesses who have been on the witness stand several times and seek improvement. Too often, I watched as expert witnesses literally put jurors to sleep. It wasn't that they didn't know their subject matter. On the contrary, they were intelligent and experienced, as a rule. The problem was their delivery.

The next time you watch the national news program, pay attention to the voices of the news anchor and reporters. Better yet, turn away from the television screen and just listen. Almost invariably, these professionals are able to keep your attention by the tone, inflection, and cadence of their speech.

While there is little you can do to change the overall tone of your voice without the help of a speech pathologist, you can work on your inflection and cadence. Inflection is simply the emphasis with which you utter words, and cadence is the speed at which they are spoken. The sure way to bore your audience is to speak in a monotone. The trick, as you discerned from listening to the news professionals, is to use variety.

Listen to a good adult reader reading a book to a group of four-year-olds. Notice how the varied inflection and cadence make the story more enjoyable. While you will not exaggerate your presentation to this degree, a more subtle demonstration of those reading skills will make your testimony more appealing.

If you are serious about improving this dimension of your presentation skills, I suggest you join an organization like Storytelling Foundation International (www.storytellingcenter.net) and learn from the real professionals. You don't have to be an actor or actress to better convey your message to juries.

Chapter Three

How to Survive Direct and Cross-Examination

Section One: What to Expect during Direct Examination

The questioning of a witness in court or in a deposition is done by direct or cross-examination. Generally speaking, direct examination is conducted by the attorney who calls the witness to the stand. Cross-examination is conducted by the attorney for a party who has not called the witness to testify. There are specific rules which govern direct, as opposed to cross, examination.

The style of questioning on direct examination parallels that used by a journalist covering a story. The attorney on direct examination or the reporter investigating a story wants to cover who, what, where, when, how and why. A very brief example of direct examination is:

Prosecutor:	Please state your name.
Witness:	My name is Jason Williams.
Prosecutor:	What is your occupation?
Witness:	I am a sergeant with the Bismarck Police Department.

Prosecutor:	Were you on duty the evening of July 3 of this year?
Witness:	Yes, I was.
Prosecutor:	Tell us where you were around 11:30 that evening.
Witness:	I was on patrol in south Bismarck when I heard a report of a domestic on Oak Street.
Prosecutor:	What did you do then?
Witness:	I called into dispatch telling them I was en route to the scene at Oak Street.
Prosecutor:	What happened next?
Witness:	When I arrived at 302 Oak Street, I saw a man stumbling across the front lawn. He appeared to have blood on his shirt and face.
Prosecutor:	What did you do then?

The cardinal rule for attorneys conducting direct examination is to let the witness fill in the answers to who, what, when, where, and how questions without suggestion from the attorney. These questions are called non-leading; they do not lead the witness to the preferred answer.

The Rules of Evidence apply at most court proceedings and at all trials. These rules specify that the attorney conducting direct examination must use non-leading questions. Rule 11 of the Federal Rules of Evidence provides:

> Leading questions should not be used on the direct examination of a witness except as may be necessary to develop the witness' testimony. Ordinarily, leading questions should be permitted on cross-examination. Whenever a party calls a hostile witness, an adverse party, or a witness identified with an adverse party, interrogation may be by leading questions.

If the attorney violates the rule by asking a leading question, opposing counsel may object to the form of the question and the judge will likely sustain the objection (agree with the attorney raising the objection) and order the question to be rephrased. Here is an example:

Prosecutor:	Where were you around 11:30 that evening?
Witness:	I was on patrol in south Bismarck when I heard a report of a domestic on Oak Street.
Prosecutor:	Did you investigate an incident at 302 Oak Street?
Witness:	Yes, I did.
Prosecutor:	When you got there, did you see a man stumbling across the front lawn, bleeding from the head?
Defense counsel:	Objection, Your Honor, counsel is leading the witness.
Judge:	Sustained. Please rephrase your question, counsel.
Prosecutor:	What did you see when you arrived at 302 Oak Street?

Note that defense counsel could also have objected to the question, "Did you investigate an incident at 302 Oak Street?" because that question was also leading. However, most courts routinely allow leading questions when they relate to preliminary matters. As another example, if the prosecutor, instead of asking the witness to state his occupation, had asked, "You're a sergeant with the Bismarck Police Department, aren't you?," the question would be leading. Nevertheless, most judges would overrule an objection and allow the question and answer to stand. Attorneys realize this and probably would not object to the question.

In short, during direct examination, the trier-of-fact hears testimony from the witness, in his or her own words. During cross-examination, the judge or jury hears a different kind of testimony. This testimony is typically an affirmation of events as worded by the attorney.

Section Two: What to Expect during Cross-Examination

> "Cross examination, the rarest, the most useful, and the most difficult to be acquired of all the accomplishments of the advocate ... It has always been deemed the surest test of truth and a better security than the oath." —Edward W. Cox

Cross-examination is at the very heart of the adversarial system. At the turn of the last century, Francis L. Wellman, in *The Art of Cross-Examination,* wrote:

> It needs but the simple statement of the nature of cross-examination to demonstrate its indispensable character in all trials of questions of fact. No cause reaches the stage of litigation unless there are two sides to it. If the witnesses on one side deny or qualify the statements made by those on the other, which side is telling the truth? Not necessarily which side is offering perjured testimony; there is far less intentional perjury in the courts than the inexperienced would believe. But which side is honestly mistaken, for, on the other hand, evidence itself is far less trustworthy than the public usually realizes. The opinions of which side are warped by prejudice or blinded by ignorance? Which side has had the power or opportunity of correct observation? How shall we tell, how make it apparent to a jury of disinterested men who are to decide between the litigants? Obviously, by the means of cross-examination.[9]

Defense counsel's basic purpose in cross-examination is to raise doubts about the accuracy of your testimony. Cross-examination can be dramatic, but as any seasoned veteran of the courtroom knows, it can also be hazardous. Too many attorneys fancy themselves to be latter-day Perry Masons only to have their case go sour because of reckless cross-examination.

In trial advocacy courses and seminars, attorneys are repeatedly warned never to ask a question on cross-examination, the answer to which they do not know with certainty. Lawyers learn, often the hard way, not to go on fishing expeditions, particularly with witnesses who are hostile. Here is a sample cross-examination where the defense attorney in a criminal case decided to go fishing.

Defense counsel:	Officer, did you see my client fleeing the scene?
Officer:	No, sir, but I subsequently observed a person matching the description of the offender running several blocks away.
Defense counsel:	Who provided you this description?
Officer:	The officer who responded to the scene.
Defense counsel:	A fellow officer provided the description of this so-called offender. Do you trust your fellow officers?
Officer:	Yes, sir, with my life.
Defense counsel:	With your life. Then let me ask you this, officer, do you have a locker room in the police station, a room where you change your clothes in preparation for your daily duties?
Officer:	Yes, sir, we do.
Defense counsel:	And do you have a locker in that room?
Officer:	Yes, sir, I do.
Defense counsel:	And do you have a lock on your locker?
Officer:	Yes, sir.
Defense counsel:	Now why is it, officer, if you trust your fellow officers with your life, that you find it necessary to lock your locker in a room you share with those same officers?
Officer:	You see, sir, we share the building with a court complex, and sometimes lawyers have been known to walk through that room.

(With that, the courtroom erupted in laughter and a prompt recess was called.)

In a typical cross-examination, questions are designed to confirm the information contained in the query. "Isn't it true that you drive a blue, four-door, Honda Accord?" Not only does the leading question put into the record information phrased exactly as desired, the technique has the additional benefit of allowing the questioner to control the witness. In most cases, questions are framed so that the only appropriate answer is "yes" or "no." While a witness is never bound to answer in this fashion, it is usually appropriate to do so.

Assume you are called to testify about a Driving While Intoxicated arrest you made. You testified on direct that, in your opinion, the driver was under the influence of intoxicating beverages. This cross-examination follows:

Defense counsel:	You say you asked my client to recite the alphabet?
Officer:	Yes, I did.
Defense counsel:	And he failed that test, you claim?
Officer:	Yes, he did.
Defense counsel:	Then you had him do the one-leg stand test?
Officer:	That's correct.
Defense counsel:	And, even though you didn't know about his old football injury, you still graded him a failure on that test?
Officer:	Yes.
Defense counsel:	Then you had him to do the heel-to-toe test?
Officer:	That's right.
Defense counsel:	And you flunked him on that one, too?
Officer:	He failed, that's correct.
Defense counsel:	But after all these tests, you still made him blow into the breathalyzer machine?
Officer:	I asked if he wanted to take the breath test.

Defense counsel:	But you already had made up your mind that he was under the influence so you gave the breath test just to hang my client, isn't that true?
Officer:	No, it's not.
Defense counsel:	You had already decided he was under the influence after he failed the first three tests, hadn't you?
Witness:	I wouldn't put it that way.
Defense counsel:	Your Honor, please instruct the witness to directly answer my question. It's a simple yes or no question.
Judge:	Please answer the question.
Witness:	I can't truthfully say "yes" to that question, Your Honor, because I don't quickly jump to conclusions.

At this point, an intelligent defense counsel will move to more fertile territory. If defense counsel persists, you may be able to inform the court that you have been involved in or heard about many cases where all kinds of excuses are made to explain bloodshot eyes, slurred speech, stumbling gait, and the like, so you are very thorough in your investigation of DWI cases just as you would be in any other kind of criminal case. The point is, you do not necessarily have to answer the question in the manner expected, "yes" or "no," if to do so would require you to violate your oath to tell the truth.

What can they ask you about? Much more than you suspect. The Rules of Evidence, followed in every court, say the cross-examiner is limited to questioning you about only those subjects touched on during direct examination. But the rule is not rigidly followed. For example, cross-examiners are generally given considerable latitude in attacking the credibility of the witness. Anything the cross-examiner can think of to question your bias, memory, or perception is fair game.

Even when the cross-examiner strays far from the subjects covered on direct examination, a judge may allow it despite an objection if the cross-examiner says: "Yes, Your Honor, I know that I've exceeded the scope of direct examination, but I ask for some latitude. Otherwise, I'll simply subpoena Mr. Olson as our witness and make him sit here for several hours until I call him to the stand. I would rather finish with him so that he might be on his way." Especially in bench trials, a judge will usually allow the cross-examiner to proceed.

If you were called upon to give an opinion during direct examination, prepare to have the basis of that opinion severely challenged. The challenge may come in several ways. First, the cross-examiner may question your expertise. This can be done by asking questions critical of your education or experience. Secondly, the cross-examiner may ask questions designed to show that you did not have all of the facts at your disposal when you arrived at your opinion, or that you based your opinion on facts assumed to be true which, in fact, were not.

The question should be rephrased: "What can't they ask you about?" The answer is, "Very little."

Section Three: How Attorneys Discredit a Witness

Since the attorney conducting cross-examination can ask leading or suggestive questions, the attorney can dictate the order in which subjects are taken up as well as the pace of the examination. Smart attorneys may begin cross-examination by inquiring into relatively innocuous or non-controversial matters. The attorney may have a friendly demeanor and give the impression that she or he and the witness are merely allies in a joint mission to seek the truth. Please be assured this is not what the attorney really has in mind. Rather, the introductory questions may be designed to curry favor with the jury and perhaps elicit some information the witness might not otherwise volunteer.

But after the attorney has squeezed all of the favorable evidence from the witness in this non-confrontational manner, the gloves come off. Now the attorney, in order to zealously represent the client, must discredit the testimony of the witness. The process of discrediting testimony is called impeachment.

The late trial advocacy expert, Irving Younger, described three common ways of impeaching a witness: showing bias or prejudice, poor memory, or poor perception. In addition to these common methods of impeachment, opposing counsel may seek to discredit a witness through the use of prior inconsistent statements, by attacking the witness's character, and by demonstrating that experts have a contrary view.[10]

Consider the following jury instruction, a variation of which is given by most courts:

Credibility of Witnesses

Another part of your duties as jurors is to decide how credible or believable each witness was. This is your duty, not mine. It is up to you to decide if a witness's testimony was believable, and how much weight you think it deserves. You are free to believe everything that a witness said, or only part of it, or none of it at all. But you should act reasonably and carefully in making these decisions.

Let me suggest some things for you to consider in evaluating each witness's testimony.

A. Ask yourself if the witness was able to clearly see or hear the events. Sometimes even an honest witness may not have been able to see or hear what was happening, and may make a mistake.

B. Ask yourself how good the witness's memory seemed to be. Did the witness seem able to accurately remember what happened?

C. Ask yourself if there was anything else that may have interfered with the witness's ability to perceive or remember the events.

D. Ask yourself how the witness acted while testifying. Did the witness appear honest? Or did the witness appear to be lying?

E. Ask yourself if the witness had any relationship to any party in this case, or anything to gain or lose from the case, that might influence the witness's testimony. Ask yourself if the witness had any bias, or prejudice, or reason for testifying that might cause the witness to lie or to slant the testimony in favor of one side or the other.

F. Ask yourself if the witness testified inconsistently while on the witness stand, or if the witness said or did something or failed to say or do something at any other time that is inconsistent with what the witness said while testifying. If you believe that the witness was inconsistent, ask yourself if this makes the witness's testimony less believable. Sometimes it may; other times it may not. Consider whether the inconsistency was about something important, or about some unimportant detail. Ask yourself if it seemed like an innocent mistake, or if it seemed deliberate.

G. And ask yourself how believable the witness's testimony was in light of all the other evidence. Was the witness's testimony supported or contradicted by other evidence that you found believable? If you believe that a witness's testimony was contradicted by other evidence, remember that people sometimes forget things, and that even two honest people who witness the same event may not describe it exactly the same way.

These are only some of the things that you may consider in deciding how believable each witness was. You may also consider other things that you think shed some light on the witness's believability. Use your common sense and your everyday experience in dealing with other people. And then decide what testimony you believe, and how much weight you think it deserves.

This jury instruction sets out quite well the various avenues of attack an attorney might take in attempting to discredit or impeach a witness.

Section Four: Impeachment by Demonstrating Prejudice or Bias

Prejudice is the holding of an opinion not based on proof or competent evidence. People typically refer to prejudice as an irrational opinion, usually negative in nature. But prejudice, which really means prejudging or judging before the fact, can be positive. For example, note the inclination of some jurors to automatically believe the testimony of clergy.

Biases, too, can be negative or positive. And while we all have biases, no one likes to admit them and we are quick to condemn, at least in our minds, those people whose biases or prejudices are exposed. This is especially true on the witness stand. One of the most potent weapons in the hands of a skilled attorney is the ability to show how a witness's perception is biased. How is this accomplished?

One way is for opposing counsel to expose a witness's educational background, training, or employment history. This is fair game. If the opposition can show that a witness is likely to sympathize with the other side because they do the same kind of work, it may impact the jury's view of the witness. Similarly, if the cross-examiner can show that years with the police force, for example, have jaded the officer's perception of anyone present at a crime scene, the officer's testimony may be impeached.

Some attorneys like to imply bias from a witness's refusal to confer with them about the case in advance of trial. This does not mean you should meet with opposing counsel before testifying. You shouldn't, unless it is by way of a deposition (See Chapter Five, Section One) or it is done with the consent and in the presence of your attorney. A defense attorney may, in a huff, inquire, "Isn't it true, Ms. Smith, that you refused to meet with me or even to talk to me about the case, when I made that request of you?" If it is true, a good response would be, "Not exactly, sir. I told you I would be happy to meet with you if the prosecutor was present, but you didn't seem interested in that."

Here is another example of how defense counsel may attempt to show bias or prejudice in court:

Defense counsel: How long have you been in law enforcement, officer?

Officer: Seven years.

Defense counsel: You've made plenty of DWI arrests before, haven't you?

Officer: Yes, I have.

Defense counsel: Hundreds?

Officer: Possibly, I don't keep count.

Defense counsel: You went through basic training to be an officer, didn't you?

Officer: Yes.

Defense counsel: And part of that training was designed to keep you and the department out of lawsuits, wasn't it?

Officer: I don't know what you mean.

Defense counsel: Well, you heard about the case where someone who was under the influence was stopped by an officer and released; then that driver hit and killed someone else and the department got sued. You didn't hear about that case?

Officer: I may have; I'm not sure.

Defense counsel: Truth is, officer, it's less risky to just take them in and book them than to let them go, isn't it?

Officer: I guess that depends.

Defense counsel: I don't want to belabor the point, officer, but isn't it true that of all the motorists you've stopped for suspected DWI, only a tiny number have been released without an arrest?

Officer: I suppose so.

Defense counsel: Don't they give awards in your department to officers who make the most DWI arrests?

Officer: I don't think so, no.

Defense counsel: But isn't there a DWI Task Force or a Mothers Against Drunk Driving group that recognizes officers who make lots of DWI arrests?

Officer: I'm not sure about that.

Defense counsel: Let's put it another way. If you came back to the station after a Saturday night shift and you hadn't made a single DWI arrest, wouldn't your shift supervisor wonder if you'd been sleeping on the job?

Officer: He might.

Defense counsel: You don't have a quota that you have to meet, do you, officer?

Officer: No, of course not.

Defense counsel: No further questions (or) Let's move on to (another subject).

There is no real antidote for this style of examination. It will almost always be permitted. Your attorney may ask some follow-up questions to "rehabilitate" you and reduce the impact of these questions addressing bias and prejudice. Do not yield to the temptation of answering, with more than a small hint of sarcasm, in this fashion:

Defense counsel: I don't want to belabor the point, officer, but isn't it true that of all the motorists you've stopped for suspected DWI, only a tiny number have been released without an arrest?

Officer: That may be true and your client was drunker than most of them.

Since you are a professional, jurors expect you to act like one. My advice is to answer these questions about bias unemotionally just as you would any others. Knowing they are coming will help in keeping your cool when you are on the witness stand.

Section Five: Impeachment by Demonstrating Poor Memory

The tactic of impeachment by showing the witness has a poor memory is used most effectively when it is difficult for the attorney to demonstrate bias or prejudice. The witness may have impeccable credentials or a reputation for honesty in the community. Under these circumstances, opposing counsel must attempt other means of impeachment.

Very few people have total recall. To make matters worse, age impairs memory. Psychologists tell us our memories operate at peak efficiency when we are about seventeen years old and it's all downhill after that. So we are prone to forget things; most jurors know this from personal experience. That is why impeachment by demonstrating poor memory is such an effective tactic.

But we shouldn't assume that simply because something happened several months or years ago, it is beyond our ability to recall it. Most baby boomers can recall exactly where they were on November 22, 1963, when President John F. Kennedy was assassinated. Our children will probably recall their place when the World Trade Center was destroyed by terrorists. Simply because an event is not fresh in time does not mean it is not fresh in memory. Ask any rape victim.

We all have constructs to help us remember things, little mental hooks we use to keep data orderly in our brains. When the triggering fact is brought to the conscious mind, the connected fact surfaces as well. Those triggers can be almost anything, a word, an image, a smell, or even the feel of something. When we are anxious, psychologists tell us, our brains do not always make the connections that occur so effortlessly in times of lower stress. I mention this to explain the common occurrence of memory lapse on the witness stand.

It's not that people are necessarily untrustworthy, although some witnesses are that, too. Rather, the drama of the courtroom heightens anxiety and causes some witnesses to freeze up on the stand. That is why good attorneys try to get the witness loosened up by asking "friendly" questions during the first few minutes of direct examination, i.e., "Are you married?" "Do you have children?" "Tell us their names and how old they are."

Not too surprisingly, some witnesses are so nervous they have trouble with even these easy questions. I can think of several instances when a witness couldn't name his children, much less their ages. A really good attorney will have taken the witness to the courtroom and staged a mock direct and cross-examination before trial. With preparation and a relaxed state of mind, the witness will respond appropriately when the real thing happens.

All of this is to presage one small piece of advice: if you can't remember something while being questioned, a good response is "I cannot remember (x) at this time." This is important because it allows the jury to infer you suffer from a temporary loss of memory, which jurors have experienced as well, rather than a lack of honesty. If they think you're dishonest, your whole testimony is not worth a tinker's damn and may actually hurt your side in the case.

Judges almost always tell jurors that if they determine a witness has intentionally lied on the stand, they may reject part or all of the witness's testimony. So it is important, if you honestly cannot remember something, to say so. What if the answer comes to you a while later? I have had situations where, several minutes after the witness said she or he couldn't remember something, the memory returned. Once, a witness said, "Judge, I just remembered the answer to Mr. Smith's question a while back. Can I answer it?" I allowed it and believe most judges would as well.

By answering, "I cannot remember at this time," the witness also gives his or her attorney the opportunity on redirect to come up with the mental hook that will release the memory. Though opposing counsel will be quick to criticize this testimony as being made up, jurors are human and recognize the frailties to which we are all subject. They know that memories are not ironclad and that the pressure of questioning under oath can cause a little slippage.

Here is an example of a cross-examination using faulty memory as an impeachment tool. The case involves a routine arrest for driving under the influence.

Defense counsel:	Was my client wearing a jacket that night?
Officer:	I believe so.
Defense counsel:	What color was it?
Officer:	Dark brown or blue, I'm not sure.
Defense counsel:	Did it have a zipper or was it a pullover?
Officer:	I think it had a zipper.
Defense counsel:	But you're not sure?
Prosecutor:	Objection, Your Honor. This is irrelevant.
Defense counsel:	Your Honor, this goes to the witness's memory and therefore his credibility.
Judge:	Overruled. Please answer the question.
Officer:	I'm not sure if it had a zipper.
Defense counsel:	Was he wearing boots, shoes, or sandals?
Officer:	Shoes, and I'm sure of that.
Defense counsel:	What kind of pants was he wearing—blue jeans, dress pants, or something else?
Officer:	Dark slacks, that's all I remember.
Defense counsel:	Was he wearing a T-shirt under his shirt?
Officer:	I couldn't say for sure.
Defense counsel:	Did he have any rings on his hands?
Officer:	I don't know.
Defense counsel:	No further questions.

While the prosecution can argue that these "memory lapses" are inconsequential, all the defense has to do is convince one of the jurors that a reasonable doubt exists because the officer's memory may be faulty. A hung jury is almost as good as an acquittal from the defendant's perspective. This is so because the new trial probably can't be rescheduled in the immediate future.

Time is usually the ally of the defendant. The more time that elapses before trial, the greater the likelihood that witnesses may move away, die, or forget the events in question. Also, if the crime is one which garners publicity, time allows the public furor to subside, for anger to diminish, and sometimes for a change of prosecutor. All of this works to the advantage of the defendant.

The best way to counter this impeachment tactic is to take better notes on the day of arrest. Memory is not like wine; it does not improve with age. It is far better to rely on good notes than on your memory.

Section Six: Impeachment by Demonstrating Lack of Perception

It is fundamental that an eyewitness cannot testify about something he or she did not see or otherwise sense. But it is also true that people's perceptions are not necessarily accurate. Some studies have shown that eyewitness identifications are accurate only slightly more than half the time.[11]

Amnesty International and other groups opposed to capital punishment cite several cases where death-row convicts have been exonerated by DNA testing after eyewitnesses convinced jurors of their guilt. Let's face it, jury trials are highly charged events and a whole host of factors can influence a verdict. I daresay a confident witness who, without hesitation, positively identifies a defendant under somewhat adverse conditions (poor lighting, short exposure, traumatic circumstances) may be at least as convincing as a less powerful witness who observed the defendant under ideal conditions.

The job of the cross-examiner is to show the jury that the witness's perception was not accurate. There are a host of ways to do this but they all rest upon the assumption that what we think we see isn't necessarily reality.

One of the ways to challenge perception is to demonstrate that the witness did not see the whole person or event, but only a piece of it. To do this, the attorney will cover several grounds. First, there is the matter of mind set. This may be tied to our biases and prejudices so an attorney may inquire about those. After implying that the witness saw what he "wanted" to see, the attorney may then move on to the witness's physical state. "How much sleep did you get the night before?" "How stressful was your day leading up to the observation in question?" "Were you under the influence of any mind-altering substances at the time?"

Next, the attorney may focus on the environment. Was it too bright, too dark, rainy, cloudy, foggy, too hot, or too cold? Anything that might affect the body's ability to effectively function is a likely subject for cross-examination. Additionally, defense counsel may inquire about any distractions that may have impaired perception.

The attorney may then turn to other visual or auditory impediments. "Do you wear glasses?" "What is your vision, uncorrected by glasses or contact lenses?" "Were you wearing sunglasses?" "Do you suffer from tinnitus or any other hearing disorder?"

Some judges will allow attorneys to perform experiments in the courtroom. Don't be surprised if an attorney wants to test your vision or hearing from the distance you claim to have seen the event in question. This is a good reason to be careful when answering questions about distance. Keep in mind how the phraseology of questions can impact the answer, e.g., "How *far* from the defendant were you when you say he struck the alleged victim?" not "How *close* were you to the defendant when you say he struck the alleged victim?" *See* Chapter Two, Section Five, Tip #3: Choose your words carefully.

Finally, in most cases, the attorney will want to show that a witness's perception was faulty because she or he had, at best, a fleeting glimpse of the subject. The direct way to do this is to focus on the element of time. If the witness had only seconds to observe the event, the attorney will harp on that fact. Another way to hone in on the short observation time is for the attorney to question the witness about other people, objects, or events attendant to the event. Did the witness notice the man behind the defendant? Did the witness notice if the window of the car was open or closed? The point, which will be made during closing argument, is that the witness's opportunity to correctly observe the event was hampered by the short time involved, as evidenced by the witness's inability to describe other people, objects, or events associated with the event.

None of this is to imply that a witness should conjure up detail that really is not in the memory bank. It is stated to show that no witness is immune from an attack on credibility. Just be forewarned that it may come and respond truthfully but without surprise or dismay.

In addition to impeachment by demonstrating bias, poor memory, or poor perception, there are other methods of attacking the credibility of a witness. One is by impeachment through prior inconsistent statements. The second is by an attack on the character of the witness. The third is by impeachment through use of a contrary view.

Section Seven: Impeachment through Prior Inconsistent Statements

When a witness testifies about facts that are very important to the case, an opponent may have proof that the witness previously made statements inconsistent with the testimony given in court. Opposing counsel will use this prior inconsistent statement to discredit the witness. Under this approach, the object is not necessarily to show that the earlier statement was true and the more recent statement false, but that any witness who is so inconsistent cannot be believed regardless of what is said or when it was said.

Even when the earlier inconsistent statement was given in the form of an opinion, most courts will allow the cross-examiner to show the jury that the testimony in court varies from that given at an earlier time. Technically speaking, the jury or judge is only supposed to consider the prior inconsistent statement for purposes of showing poor credibility, not to prove the matter asserted in the earlier statement. But juries seldom make such fine distinctions. So if the witness, on an earlier occasion, gave the opinion that Peter Campbell was intoxicated but now says Peter was fairly sober, the jury may well believe the earlier statement. Alternatively, the jury can simply disregard both statements of the witness choosing to believe neither.

How is impeachment through prior inconsistent statements carried out? There are two methods. One is to call another witness or other witnesses to testify that an earlier inconsistent statement was made.

Defense counsel:	Miss Kramer, you heard Officer Johnson testify today that he thought my client, Peter Campbell, was drunk on November 8?
Witness:	Yes, I did.
Defense counsel:	Have you known Officer Johnson long?
Witness:	For about two years.
Defense counsel:	Have you ever talked to him about the incident on November 8?
Witness:	Yes, we talked about it a few days after it happened.
Defense counsel:	Back in November?
Witness:	Yes.
Defense counsel:	What did Officer Johnson say back then?
Witness:	He said Mr. Campbell was a pain in the you-know-what, but he wasn't drunk.
Defense counsel:	Thank you, Miss Kramer. I have no further questions.

The second method is to have the witness who is being impeached admit the prior inconsistent statement during cross-examination. This method, if done properly, can be fairly dramatic.

Defense counsel:	Officer, you testified on direct that my client staggered when he walked on September 20.

Officer:	Yes, that's right.
Defense counsel:	You seem most certain of that today.
Officer:	I'm certain, yes.
Defense counsel:	The events you've testified to today took place several months ago, isn't that correct?
Officer:	That's true.
Defense counsel:	Would you say that, like the rest of us, your memory of recent events is somewhat better than your memory of older events?
Officer:	I suppose so.
Defense counsel:	For example, you can probably remember what you ate for dinner yesterday but would have a hard time remembering what you ate, say, on September 20 of last year?
Officer:	I'd agree with that.
Defense counsel:	Now, in your position as a peace officer, you document many of the things you do, right?
Officer:	Yes.
Defense counsel:	That's important for a lot of reasons, isn't it, officer?
Officer:	Sure.
Defense counsel:	I mean it's important to your supervisor to show you're doing your job correctly?
Officer:	Yes.
Defense counsel:	And it's important to the prosecutor so they have an accurate account of what you did when you made an arrest?
Officer:	Yes.

Defense counsel: So you do your very best to be thorough in documenting things?

Officer: I try to be, yes.

Defense counsel: And you certainly want your reports to be accurate?

Officer: Of course.

Defense counsel: Did you prepare a report after you arrested my client?

Officer: Yes, I did.

Defense counsel: How many pages long is it?

Officer: Two pages.

Defense counsel: And this was prepared when?

Officer: The same night I arrested him.

Defense counsel: So it was only minutes after the event?

Officer: Within an hour or two.

Defense counsel: When your memory was fresh?

Officer: Yes.

Defense counsel: May I approach the witness, Your Honor?

Judge: Yes, you may.

Defense counsel: I show you a two-page document entitled "Officer Report." Do you recognize it?

Officer: Yes, it's a copy of my report.

Defense counsel: And this is the kind of report you testified earlier that you strive very hard to make accurate and thorough?

Officer: Yes.

Defense counsel: I'd like you to read through your report silently, officer—please take your time—then read out loud the portion of your report where you say my client staggered.

(Pause)

Defense counsel:	Well?
Officer:	It's not there.
Defense counsel:	Of course not. Then read to us the second sentence in the eighth paragraph, the one I have highlighted in yellow.
Officer:	"The subject got into the squad car without difficulty."
Defense counsel:	No further questions, Your Honor.

Sometimes, defense counsel will have taken a deposition of the witness before trial. If the witness said something at trial that differs significantly from the testimony given at the deposition, the attorney will bring this out on cross-examination.

Attorney:	Mr. Jones, am I correct in understanding that your testimony today is that the light was green when the Ford Bronco entered the intersection on July 4?
Witness:	Yes, that's right.
Attorney:	You are sure about that?
Witness:	Yes, I am.
Attorney:	And you are telling us the truth, aren't you?
Witness:	Of course.
Attorney:	If anyone had ever asked you after July 4, what color the traffic signal was as the Ford Bronco entered that intersection, you would have said "green," isn't that correct?
Witness:	Yes.
Attorney:	As a truthful person with a clear recall of the collision on July 4, you would never had said anything other than that the Ford Bronco had the green light, correct?
Witness:	No, of course not.

Attorney:	(picks up a copy of the deposition but does not show it to the witness) Mr. Jones, do you remember giving a deposition in this case on February 20?
Witness:	Yes.
Attorney:	At that deposition, you answered some questions about the collision on July 4, didn't you?
Witness:	Yes, I did.
Attorney:	You took an oath to tell the truth at that deposition, didn't you?
Witness:	Yes.
Attorney:	That was an oath just like the one you took today, wasn't it?
Witness:	Yes, it was.
Attorney:	And you told the truth at your deposition, didn't you?
Witness:	Yes, I did.
Attorney:	That deposition was taken only a few months after the collision, right?
Witness:	That's right.
Attorney:	You still had a good memory of the collision when you testified at your deposition on February 20, didn't you?
Witness:	Yes.
Attorney:	(Opens the transcript to a page without showing it to the witness) Mr. Jones, at your deposition weren't you asked what color the traffic light was when the Ford Bronco entered the intersection? (to opposing counsel: "You will find it at page 24, line 5.")
Witness:	Yes, I think you asked me about that.

Attorney:	And in response to that question, isn't it true that you stated the light was red?
Witness:	No, I don't think I said that.
Attorney:	Let the record reflect that I am showing opposing counsel what has been marked as Exhibit 9 for identification. (Hands deposition to opposing counsel for examination)
Attorney:	Your Honor, may I approach the witness?
Judge:	Yes, you may.
Attorney:	(Counsel approaches the witness) Now, Mr. Jones, you recognize this exhibit, don't you?
Witness:	Yes.
Attorney:	Isn't this a transcript of the deposition you gave on February 20?
Witness:	I guess so.
Attorney:	Look at it carefully. Doesn't it show that you reviewed it for accuracy?
Witness:	Yes.
Attorney:	And you signed it indicating that it was accurate?
Witness:	Yes.
Attorney:	Let me direct your attention to page 24, starting at line 5. (attorney points to the page and line in the transcript) Isn't it true that, at your deposition, you were asked, "What color was the light when the Ford Bronco entered the intersection?"
Witness:	Yes.
Attorney:	Isn't it also true that in response to that question, your sworn testimony was, "The light was red."

Witness:	Yes, that's what it says.
Attorney:	No further questions.

Here is another example of impeachment through a prior inconsistent statement given at a deposition:

Attorney:	Officer Smith, you say that when you investigated the accident you noticed ten feet of skid marks directly behind the location where the defendant's Ford came to a stop?
Witness:	That is correct.
Attorney:	Do you recall giving a deposition in my office last June where we questioned you about this matter?
Witness:	Yes, I do.
Attorney:	Do you recall that the prosecutor was present at the deposition and that a court reporter was taking down everything we said?
Witness:	Yes.
Attorney:	You were put under oath, you raised your right hand, and you swore to tell the truth that day, didn't you?
Witness:	Yes, I did.
Attorney:	And you told the truth then, didn't you?
Witness:	Yes.
Attorney:	At that deposition, I told you up front that if any of my questions were confusing or if you did not understand a question, you should simply let me know and I would rephrase it. Do you remember that?
Witness:	Yes.
Attorney:	And you told me that you would let me know if you didn't understand a question, didn't you?

Witness:	Yes.
Attorney:	Before you came to my office for that deposition, you discussed what questions I might ask with the prosecutor, didn't you?
Witness:	Yes.
Attorney:	After you gave your answers under oath with your lawyer present, the questions and answers were typed out and given to you to read over to see if they were accurate, right?
Witness:	Yes, that's right.
Attorney:	And, in fact, you did read the questions and answers and you signed the deposition on the last page under oath before a notary indicating that everything was accurately recorded, correct?
Witness:	Yes.
Attorney:	Would it be fair to say that your memory of the accident last June was better and fresher on the day of your deposition than it is today?
Witness:	I suppose so.
Attorney:	Now, Officer Smith, at your deposition, under oath, with your lawyer present, weren't you asked the following question and didn't you give the following answer: "Question—After you arrived at the scene of the accident, did you see any skid marks? Answer—No, I looked all around but didn't see any." That's what you said, isn't it?
Witness:	If it's in there, I must have said it.

There is no good way to thwart impeachment by use of a prior inconsistent statement. The lesson: don't make them in the first place.

Section Eight: Impeachment by Use of a Contrary View

An effective method of discrediting a witness's testimony is to show that the witness's opinion or activity differs from that of leading experts. The jury is informed, through cross-examination, that the witness's views are wrong or their actions inappropriate.

For example, in a DWI case, if you administered the walk-and-turn and counting backwards field sobriety tests, defense counsel may imply you should have used the one-legged stand and alphabet tests. If you used the one-legged stand and alphabet tests, defense counsel may imply you should have used the walk-and-turn and counting backwards tests. It's a tactic many defense attorneys use, often effectively.

Section Nine: Impeachment by Attack on Character

Probably the least commonly used method of impeaching a witness is by an attack on character. Nevertheless, it is important to know of all possible means by which the opposition can discredit testimony.

Conviction of a Crime

One way to attack character is to show evidence that the witness has been convicted of a crime. This attack is allowed on the theory that criminals, generally, are untrustworthy. The courts in various states have different standards for determining what kinds of crimes are permissible subjects for impeachment purposes. Most do not allow a witness to be impeached with evidence of misdemeanors unless they involve dishonesty or false statement. Almost all courts will permit impeachment by revelation of a felony. Misdemeanors are generally those offenses carrying a maximum sentence of imprisonment for one year or less.

Impeachment through evidence of a criminal conviction is limited in scope. Most courts will allow the impeaching attorney to ask a witness for the name of the crime, the time and place of conviction, and the punishment. Details, such as the name of the victim and any aggravating circumstances, may not be inquired into. Convictions more than ten years old are generally not admissible.

Evidence of a witness's criminal record can be introduced through the witness or by extrinsic evidence, or by both means. The impeaching attorney usually asks the witness the particulars of the crime with the limitations described above. Then the attorney typically introduces, as an exhibit, a certified copy of the judgment of conviction.

The use of a witness's prior criminal record to discredit testimony is but one of the reasons why law enforcement agencies screen applicants thoroughly and have a low tolerance for dishonesty on the job. The officer's value to the agency can be greatly compromised by any criminal conviction.

Character for Untruthfulness

A second way to impeach is to demonstrate a character for untruthfulness. This is done, not by questioning the witness who is impeached, but by soliciting testimony from others who know the witness.

Attorney:	Do you know the general reputation in this community of James Smith for truth and veracity?
Witness:	Yes, I do.
Attorney:	What is that reputation?
Witness:	It is not very good, I'm afraid.

The witness is not allowed to recite specific instances of untruthful conduct or to give the witness's own opinion of Smith's veracity. Only Smith's reputation in the community is admissible, and then limited to his character for truthfulness. In other words, the impeachment cannot stray to community reputation for laziness, sexual misconduct, or any of a host of other bad traits.

Section Ten: Some Tips for Testifying on Cross-Examination

Now you know some of the methods defense attorneys use to discredit witness's testimony. Here are some tips for enhancing your credibility in the eyes of the jury and judge.

Tip #1: Don't volunteer

> "If you don't say anything, you won't be called upon to repeat it."
> —Calvin Coolidge

Skillful cross-examiners will phrase their questions in such a manner that your answers are limited to "yes," "no," or some other short response. Occasionally, though, opposing counsel will go "fishing." This typically happens when the attorney surmises that your response will not hurt, and may help, the cross-examiner's cause no matter what it is.

You should be especially cautious in these circumstances. Do not volunteer anything more than necessary in response to the question. Also, be sure you know exactly what the attorney is seeking before you respond. Sometimes, the attorney does not even know what he or she is fishing for and simply wants to give you an opportunity to help.

Defense counsel:	Then you arrested my client and hauled him to jail?
Officer:	Yes, that's right.
Defense counsel:	Before you left the scene, was there anything else that you observed? or Did anything else happen before you got back to the station? or What else did you notice about my client?

It is proper, under these circumstances, to say, "I'm not sure I understand what it is you are asking. Could you be more specific?"

If the attorney becomes indignant and demands that you answer the question as initially phrased, you can respond that vague questions are hard to answer (this is also an alert to your attorney that an objection for vagueness may be appropriate) but that if the court is not pressed for time, you'd be willing to address the question at length. At this point, most judges will sustain an objection to vagueness or ask the attorney to rephrase the question.

Remember, you will never persuade opposing counsel to your point of view, so don't fall into the trap of thinking that giving a long, rambling answer is going to win over anyone. Remember that jurors are looking forward to the next recess. They don't relish listening to more testimony than necessary, especially when it doesn't seem particularly important. Rambling carries with it the danger that some small part of the testimony may be used by the opposition later to discredit your testimony.

Don't volunteer information during direct examination, either. You may think that certain information which you possess should be heard by the jury despite the fact that your attorney has not asked you for it. Be careful! It is possible the "extra" information you mention has been the subject of a pre-trial motion and the judge has ruled it is inadmissible. If you blurt out this inadmissible information at trial, the defense may ask for a mistrial which makes the prosecution look bad in the eyes of some jurors. Worse, the judge may grant the motion and you will be back to square one with a new trial, months later.

If there is a recess during your testimony, feel free to discuss your concern with your attorney. Tell the prosecutor you think you have information which hasn't been brought out on the witness stand. It can be covered after the recess. Even if you have finished testifying, you should still point out the omitted information to the prosecutor when you next get the chance. There is the possibility you could be recalled as a witness if the prosecutor thought it necessary. But don't flirt with danger by volunteering information that has not been solicited by your attorney.

Tip #2: Keep your options open

Most witnesses are fact witnesses, that is, witnesses who relate to the jury or judge the details of something they did or observed. Fact witnesses tend to be questioned closely about the activity or observation. If you are a fact witness, be careful in your response not to hem yourself in by saying such things as, "That was all of the conversation," or "Nothing else happened," unless you are absolutely sure of your memory.

Even when you think you recall an incident clearly, you may have forgotten certain details. With prodding, you may remember much more than you thought possible. Also, you may never have consciously noted everything that happened in the first place. Months later under oath, it is often difficult to say with certainty what happened.

The better response is to say, "That is all of the conversation I can recall at this time," or "That is all I remember right now about what happened that day." Then, if something comes to mind or is brought to your attention later, you are safe.

Tip #3: Clarify, if necessary

Assume you were asked a question earlier by one of the attorneys and you now realize the answer you gave was incorrect. What should you do? You could wait until you are done testifying and then tell your attorney about it at the next recess. The attorney could then ask the court's permission to recall you to the stand so that the correction can be made.

There are two problems with this approach. First, jurors may wonder what is so important about the testimony that it deserves recalling you to the stand. It may not be the best strategy to go back over it so your attorney may choose not to bring it to the court's attention. Secondly, the judge may not allow you to be recalled to the stand, determining that the testimony is only marginally relevant and would consume too much time to address.

But if you don't clarify the mistake you made, there is the risk that the defense will learn about it and exploit it to the defendant's advantage. You don't want this to happen. My advice is to do what most people do in their conversations: correct the mistake as soon as you realize it. You can make the correction at the end of your answer to a question.

Attorney:	When did you talk to Mr. Jones?
Witness:	That would have been on March 3. (Turn to the judge) Your Honor, when I was asked a little while ago about where I bought the car, I said it was at Hansen's Ford but I just remembered that I bought it at Schlenker's A-1 Used Cars. I thought you should know that.

The judge will likely not respond to your "correction" and simply ask the cross-examiner to continue with the next question. If the judge or cross-examiner cuts you off before you finish your correction, you will have alerted your attorney that the matter needs to be addressed and you can be fairly certain your attorney will deal with it, *before* you leave the witness stand.

(on redirect examination)

Your attorney:	You said something about the place you bought the car?
Witness:	Yes, I was mistaken earlier when I said I bought it at Hansen's Ford. That was a different car. The one in question was purchased at Schlenker's A-1 Used Cars.

Jurors appreciate honesty. When you've made a mistake, admit it candidly and promptly. Your credibility will likely improve in the eyes of the fact-finder, whether jury or judge.

Tip #4: Stop when there is an objection

Often during cross-examination, your attorney will object to a question put to you by opposing counsel. When this happens, stop! No matter what you were saying or how crucial you believe it is to the case, do not speak further until the objection has been ruled upon. Do not even finish your sentence.

As a matter of court procedure, the judge must rule upon an objection unless the cross-examiner withdraws the question or the objecting attorney withdraws the objection. Sometimes, one of the attorneys will want to make an argument about the objection outside the hearing of the jury. The judge may call the attorneys up to the bench where they can be heard by the judge but not by the jurors. Less frequently, an objection may involve complex legal issues that require more time to resolve. The judge may take a recess while the issue is hammered out in chambers.

But whether the decision of the judge takes several minutes or only a few seconds to make, you should wait before answering. Unless the judge prohibits it, you may listen to the arguments made during a bench conference. It is sometimes helpful to hear what the controversy is about when pondering how best to answer the question. However, jurors may not know that it is proper for you to "eavesdrop" on the bench conference, so try not to make it obvious.

Tip #5: Explain technical terms immediately

Witnesses need to keep in mind that the average juror has a high school education, and many have less than that. When testifying, it is important that your words are clearly understood. This does not mean that you must abandon any vocabulary foreign to the general public. What it does imply is that you should use only those terms you are prepared to define immediately after they are spoken. Here is an example:

Prosecutor: Officer, why did you go to 907 Oak Street?

Officer: Dispatch reported a 10-16 at that location; by that I mean a staff person called me and reported there was a family dispute at 907 Oak Street.

If you fail to explain terms, the jury may not follow the rest of your testimony or worse, think you're arrogant for "talking over their heads." The best practice is to explain terms by way of example or analogy. Give this some thought before you get on the stand. You will be pleasantly surprised at how much technical knowledge a jury can absorb if it is broken down into digestible parts and explained through examples.

Tip #6: Beware of the "Isn't it possible" question

While judges should not allow questions which ask the witness to speculate, in practice, many of the "Isn't it possible ..." questions slip through without objection. That means you have to answer them.

Defense counsel: Isn't it possible my client's eyes were red as a result of his allergies?
or
Isn't it possible the alleged victim struck my client first?

You can try to avoid them with the response, "I'd like to answer that question but my answer would be a sheer guess." This should prompt an objection and, most likely, a ruling from the judge that you do not have to answer the question.

If you do address the substance of the question, you can say, if you believe it is true, "Almost anything under the sun is possible, so I cannot say there is zero chance of it being true, but I think it is highly doubtful."

Tip #7: Be careful about questions involving time and distance

A frequent technique employed by the cross-examiner is to suggest distances or times and hope that you will adopt them. This can lead to problems later. Often the witness won't realize they've played into the cross-examiner's hands until final summation when the witness's testimony is recalled for the jury.

Defense counsel: Your report says that you stopped my client at 2:45 a.m. What was the first thing you did after he pulled to a stop?

Officer:	I asked him for his license and registration.
Defense counsel:	You first had to get out of your squad car, walk up to his car, and he had to roll down the window, correct?
Officer:	Oh, sure, that's right.
Defense counsel:	And how long did that take?
Officer:	Not very long, may a few minutes.
Defense counsel:	Three minutes or so?
Officer:	I suppose.
Defense counsel:	Then you talked to him, waited for him to give you the documentation, got it, and returned to your squad car, right?
Officer:	Yes.
Defense counsel:	And that took another three to five minutes, would you say?
Officer:	I suppose so.
Defense counsel:	Then what did you do next?
Officer:	I called in and did a records check on the license of the vehicle.
Defense counsel:	And you had to wait for them to do that records check and report back to you; that took another three to five minutes?
Officer:	Sure.

(defense counsel continues through every detail of the officer's activity, exaggerating the length of time each consumed)

Defense counsel:	May we approach the bench Your Honor?
Judge:	Yes, you may.
Defense counsel:	(at the bench conference) Your Honor, we move to dismiss the complaint. In this state, an officer must administer the breath or blood test to a suspect within

	two hours of detaining him or the test result is inadmissible. By my calculations, adding up the times testified to by the officer, it was two hours and fifteen minutes from the time my client was stopped until testing. The breath test should be thrown out. Without the breath test, there is no case against my client.
Judge:	Your point is well taken. The breath test is out. Mr. Prosecutor, do you have other evidence you think will sustain a guilty verdict, because if you don't, I plan to take a recess. Maybe you two can work out a plea bargain satisfactory to both sides. (The prosecutor groans inaudibly.)

Tip #8: Pay attention to "buzzwords"

In many cases, the defense in the case hinges on whether the defendant had the necessary state of mind to commit the crime. There are words, called legal terms of art, which have specific meaning in court. Some of them are "intent," "mistake," "negligent" and "reckless." When these words are used in the context of a question from a cross-examining attorney, pay close attention. These questions go to the very heart of the case. Be sure of your answer before saying anything which you may have to qualify or correct later.

Defense counsel:	Officer, you're not saying my client was reckless when the cars collided, are you?
Officer:	That's not for me to say. All I can tell you is what my measurements showed and what the damage to the vehicles was.

Chapter Four

Expert Testimony

Section One: How to Give Opinion Testimony

The Rules of Evidence allow expert witnesses to give an opinion about matters within their areas of expertise. For example, a police officer can give an opinion about whether or not a motorist was under the influence of intoxicating liquor.

Who is an expert? Anyone who, as a result of education, training, or experience, possesses information that would be helpful to the jury or judge in understanding the matter at hand. It is not necessary that an expert have a college degree or even a high school diploma. All that is required is a significant knowledge base in the subject area at issue in the trial.

Typically, the opinion is elicited during direct examination:

Attorney:	Officer, after you concluded your field sobriety tests, did you form an opinion about whether Arthur Thompson was under the influence of intoxicating beverages?
Witness:	Yes, I did.
Attorney:	What is your opinion?
Witness:	I believe he was under the influence.

A good attorney will always ask, "Do you have an opinion?" before asking, "What is your opinion?" Thus, you will have advance notice that the ultimate question is coming. In many trials, this testimony is at the very heart of the case. It will boost credibility if you have planned in advance exactly how you will answer the opinion question.

A typical follow-up question is, "On what do you base your opinion?" This will usually allow you to restate portions of your earlier testimony and give support for your opinion. In jury trials, psychologists tell us, repetition is key to getting jurors to remember testimony. These professionals advise attorneys, "In your opening statement, tell the jury the important fact which you will present to them during the trial, follow through by having witnesses relate these facts, and then, in closing argument, summarize the testimony or tell them what you've told them."

Again, it is helpful if you plan how you will answer the follow-up question, "On what do you base your opinion?" Your response should be thorough but succinct. Don't bore the jury with a repetition of everything you've previously told them, but summarize the facts which point inevitably to the conclusion you reached.

Section Two: Qualifying the Witness as an Expert

In order for the prosecution to use your opinion as evidence in a case, you must be "qualified" as an expert. The qualification is not as difficult as you may think. Bearing in mind that anyone with sufficient training or experience can be an expert, the prosecutor's questions will simply probe your background to show that you know what you're testifying about. Here is an example from a Driving While Intoxicated case.

Prosecutor: Would you tell us your name please?

Officer: Sergeant Mike White.

Prosecutor:	Where do you work?
Officer:	I'm with the Standing Rock Police Department.
Prosecutor:	How long have you worked there?
Officer:	This is my seventh year.
Prosecutor:	Did you have any law enforcement experience before coming to Standing Rock?
Officer:	Yes, I worked for three years at the Crow Creek Reservation in South Dakota.
Prosecutor:	What training have you had?
Officer:	I have an Associate of Arts degree from Bismarck State College and completed the sixteen-week basic training course at the Law Enforcement Training Academy in Bismarck. I've also attended many seminars and conferences over the last ten years that covered most every aspect of law enforcement.
Prosecutor:	Have you had training specifically in the area of detecting impaired drivers?
Officer:	Yes, I've had numerous training sessions about DWI, including a lengthy segment during basic training.
Prosecutor:	Over the past ten years, have you made arrests for Driving While Intoxicated or being in Actual Physical Control of a motor vehicle while under the influence?
Officer:	Oh, yes.
Prosecutor:	Could you estimate the number of arrests you've made?
Officer:	It would be in the hundreds.
Prosecutor:	And can I assume that you investigated some cases where you determined the driver was *not* under the influence?

Officer:	Yes, there have been several of those also.
Prosecutor:	Any estimate of how many?
Officer:	I would say dozens, but probably less than fifty.
Prosecutor:	Do you or any of your family or friends consume alcoholic beverages?
Officer:	Yes, I do on occasion, as do several of my friends and family.
Prosecutor:	Then you've seen people you know well when they're sober and again after drinking?
Officer:	Sure.
Prosecutor:	So you've seen the effects of alcohol used in moderation?
Officer:	Yes.
Prosecutor:	You've also seen people you know who have had too much to drink?
Officer:	Yes.
Prosecutor:	And you're able to compare them to when they are sober?
Officer:	I think so, yes.
Prosecutor:	[asks questions about the circumstances leading to the arrest of the defendant] Based on your training and experience, Officer White, do you have an opinion as to whether or not the defendant was under the influence on the night you arrested him?
Officer:	Yes, I do.
Prosecutor:	What is that opinion?
Officer:	I believe he was under the influence of intoxicating liquor that night.

There are limits to an officer's expertise and you should be careful to stay within them. For example, an officer may come upon a motorist slumped over behind the wheel of a vehicle and see an open container of an alcoholic beverage inside. Most officers would assume the driver is passed out from the alcohol because this is a fairly common occurrence. At trial, the examination on direct and cross may go like this:

Prosecutor:	When you shined your flashlight inside the defendant's car, what did you notice?
Officer:	I saw the driver slumped over, unconscious, behind the wheel, and an open bottle of beer on the floorboard by his feet.
Defense counsel:	Objection, Your Honor! May I ask just a few questions to lay the foundation for my objection?
Judge:	Yes, you may.
Defense counsel:	Officer, are you a licensed physician?
Officer:	No.
Defense counsel:	A physician's assistant?
Officer:	No.
Defense counsel:	A registered nurse?
Officer:	No.
Defense counsel:	What medical degree or certification do you possess?
Officer:	None.
Defense counsel:	Your Honor, I renew my objection to the witness's opinion that my client was unconscious. He has no training from which to conclude that my client wasn't asleep, or conscious but resting his eyes, or anything else. He simply doesn't have the qualifications to be making these rash assumptions.

Judge:	Sustained. The jury will disregard the officer's opinion.

In this scenario, the witness loses credibility. You do not want a judge telling a jury to disregard any of your testimony, ever. Be cognizant when using medical terms. A better way to make the point is simply to state the facts with attention given to detail. Here is another way of answering the same question.

Prosecutor:	When you shined your flashlight inside the defendant's car, what did you notice?
Officer:	I saw the driver slumped over behind the wheel, and an open bottle of beer on the floorboard by his feet.
Prosecutor:	What did you do then?
Officer:	I rapped on the window to get his attention but got no response. It was cold out and I had gloves on, so I took off my right glove and rapped again, even louder, but still got no response. I then knocked a third time, even harder, so hard my knuckles hurt, and he didn't seem to notice.

It is far better, in most cases, to allow the facts to speak for themselves. Let the judge and jury draw their own conclusions. They will invariably reach the same one you did. Trust them.

Section Three: When Not to Give an Opinion

If you are not asked for an opinion, don't give it. If your attorney wants you to give an opinion, the issue will usually be discussed before trial. But it is dangerous to offer an opinion when one has not been solicited unless there is solid evidence *in the record* to support it. You may have an opinion based, at least in part, on information which has not been produced at trial. Your opinion will be attacked and may be discredited by the opposition under these circumstances. You are best advised not to give an opinion unless you have given the supporting evidence yourself.

In bench trials, another reason you do not want to offer unsolicited opinions is that the judge wants to make the ultimate decision based on facts. The judge needs facts more than your opinion as to what the facts show, in order to make a rational decision. "That's what they pay me to do," one judge quipped after rendering a verdict contrary to the opinion offered by an expert witness. This is especially true with issues that are seen frequently in court. More deference is given to an expert's opinion in matters of science or other areas not routinely heard in court.

Chapter Five

What You Need to Know about Depositions

Section One: What Is a Deposition?

A deposition is a process by which a witness is required to answer questions under oath. Almost all depositions are taken well in advance of trial. In the vast majority of criminal cases, neither side will take depositions. But if the defendant has the financial ability, defense counsel may take the depositions of key witnesses who will testify for the prosecution. In civil cases, depositions of key witnesses are the norm.

There are two reasons, set forth in the rules, for taking depositions. One is to preserve evidence for trial, and the other is for discovery purposes.

An example of a deposition taken to preserve evidence is taking the sworn statement of a terminally ill person who may not live to testify at trial. This kind of deposition is taken when a witness cannot, for bona fide reasons, attend a hearing or trial, or when both sides agree that a deposition may be used instead of live testimony at trial. The questions asked and answers given during the deposition may become part of the record at trial when a reader takes the stand and substitutes for the witness. The reader recites questions and answers verbatim from a transcript of the deposition.

The more common reason for taking a deposition, especially in civil cases, is for discovery. It allows the opposing party to find out, in advance of trial, what the witness is likely to say on the witness stand. This kind of deposition is rarely used at trial if the witness is there to testify in person but excerpts from the deposition can be used for impeachment purposes.

What does the opposing attorney want to discover? Everything you know about the case and how well you can communicate it to a jury at trial. Through a deposition, counsel can evaluate the strengths and weaknesses of the case, prevent surprises at trial, pin down testimony on particular points, determine if standard tests or procedures were followed, and gain favorable admissions. Depositions are also used to check for biases on the part of witnesses.

Depositions are generally held in the law office of the attorney who schedules it or in some neutral place, but almost never in a courthouse. Notice of the time, place, and date of the deposition is given to the witness by means of a subpoena. This legal order requiring the witness to appear is often signed by the opponent's attorney, not by a judge. This is permissible under the rules.

The attorney may also choose to issue a *subpoena duces tecum* which not only commands the presence of the witness for the deposition but requires the witness to bring certain documents to the session. As a general rule, you should not volunteer for a deposition. If there is no subpoena, you do not have to submit to a deposition.

Judges rarely attend depositions. There are exceptions for cases where numerous significant objections to testimony are anticipated, especially in cases involving child witnesses or allegedly confidential information. But in most cases, those present at the deposition include the attorneys, the witness, and a court reporter. The court reporter administers an oath to the witness and then makes a record of everything said. The court reporter also keeps track of any exhibits that are used during the deposition. Sometimes, a paralegal or legal assistant will also attend the deposition.

Because judges are typically absent from depositions, when an objection to a question is made, there is no immediate ruling allowing or disallowing the question. As a practical matter then, the witness answers the question even though an objection has been made. Later, if the matter is significant enough to be brought to the trial judge's attention, the answer may be determined inadmissible. It is permissible for you to look to your attorney for advice when she or he raises an objection to a question. Unless directed by your attorney not to answer a question, you should answer it even though an objection has been raised.

Section Two: I'm Going to Be Deposed. Now What?

Everything stated earlier in this book about testifying generally holds true for depositions. But there are some additional things to keep in mind.

1. Work with your attorney to reschedule the deposition if it creates a conflict for you. There is nothing sacred about the date and time selected by opposing counsel.
2. Prepare for the deposition by reviewing your records and reports. It is always a good idea to meet with your attorney to discuss the deposition. Ask your attorney what the crucial issues are and if your opinion will likely be solicited. Also ask your attorney if other potential witnesses have been subpoenaed for deposition. If so, determine who they are and, if they have already been deposed, what they said. This will give you a good idea of the subjects likely to be focused on by opposing counsel.
3. Be ready to tell what you did to prepare for the deposition. A standard question asked at depositions is "What documents did you review and with whom did you meet to prepare for this deposition?" Give an accurate, thorough response to the question. If asked, "Is that everything you reviewed?" give yourself some leeway by answering, "That is all that I can think of right now."

4. Unless required by *subpoena duces tecum*, however, do not bring any files or records with you to the deposition. Anything you bring is subject to examination by opposing counsel so do not bring anything more than is absolutely necessary. In reviewing your file, you may come across "damaging" memos or other documents. Do not throw these away. While you do not have to bring them to the deposition unless they are requested, it is improper to destroy them. Aside from the serious legal and ethical concerns, if a judge or jury learns that you destroyed evidence, your credibility will suffer immeasurably.

5. Be candid. If something is asked which is personally embarrassing, answer truthfully and completely. Better that it comes out at the deposition than at trial when it may be too late to counter it or keep it from becoming an issue. Depositions often involve a fair amount of "fishing" for information favorable to the angler.

6. Avoid humor. The setting for a deposition is much less formal than at trial and witnesses have a tendency to let down their guard. This informality may be fostered and encouraged by opposing counsel. There are two dangers lurking for the complacent witness. First, the witness may divulge information that should not have been revealed. Second, humor does not come across well on paper. When a particular passage is read to a jury, words that brought peals of laughter in the lawyer's office fall flat in the courtroom.

7 Pause before answering. Think about the question and gather your thoughts before launching into an answer. This also gives your attorney time to make an objection. The record, unless videotaped, does not reflect short pauses so it does not hurt to take a little extra time in formulating your response.

8. Beware of the pregnant pause. At depositions, opposing counsel may ask a vague question, not knowing the precise terminology to put into the form of the question, then fumble about or pause, hoping you will "fill in the blanks." This is particularly true of the attorney who has not done much background research and is unfamiliar with a subject. Do not help. It is not your job to educate opposing counsel.

9. Don't be obstinate. While no one wants to concede points unnecessarily, there are times when you can and should overlook minor flaws in a question. So long as you can do so while making a truthful answer, you should avoid petty skirmishes. Arguing over minor details diminishes your credibility.
10. The most credible answers to questions for which you do not know the answer are "I don't know" or "I do not remember at this time." By including "at this time," you allow for the possibility that something might jog your memory of the event.
11. Don't volunteer information. We all know people who, if asked "What time is it?," respond by telling the questioner how to build a clock. These people are asking for trouble at a deposition. Do not give more information than is required to honestly answer the question. The more detail you offer, the broader the area opposing counsel will want to cover with additional questions. Unless you have a masochistic bent, you will want the deposition to end as quickly as possible. Giving elaborate answers is a sure-fire way to stretch out a deposition.
12. Take a break. Some depositions may last several hours. It is permissible to ask for, or even to insist upon, a break. During the break do not converse with opposing counsel or anyone associated with them about anything even remotely connected to the case. This includes the inquisitive paralegal who is working for the opposition. Remember, this is not a social occasion.
13. Avoid lengthy statements. Do not try to convince opposing counsel by engaging in long-winded arguments and explanations intended to persuade. They make you look weak and turn juries off.
14. Never make a comment "off the record." There may be some preliminary discussion but the actual deposition begins when the court reporter administers the oath to the witness. From that point forward, every word is recorded and is potential evidence to be used later at trial. Before the deposition, or during a break, opposing counsel may bring up an issue which you are inclined to address. Hold your tongue. Whether or not opposing counsel has done this deliberately or simply as part of social

conversation, if your response is helpful to the other side, rest assured it will be brought out "on the record" either during the deposition or at trial.

15. Be careful not to use head nods or "uh-huhs" or "um-hmm" as answers. They do not translate well in print. There is at least a fair possibility that some of your deposition testimony will be read to a jury at trial.

16. Different rules apply at video depositions. When you are scheduled for a deposition, the notice will tell you whether or not your testimony will be videotaped. If the notice does not give you this information, ask your attorney. This is important. If this is a videotaped deposition, all of the rules about dress, appearance, and nonverbal communication apply. You may even want to use light makeup (even if you are a male) to make you more appealing to the viewer who will not know you used makeup. Talk to someone with experience in the video field for advice. You cannot pause long before answering on videotape without looking unsure of yourself or evasive. This may mean more preparation is necessary before the deposition. Don't chew gum, gnaw on a pen, or do anything else which is distracting. Look straight at the questioner and exude confidence and sincerity. If you refer to an exhibit while testifying, be sure it can be seen on camera. You may feel a bit like an actor doing a television commercial holding a candy bar next to your cheek while you talk, but if that's what it takes to make your testimony clear, so be it. Practice with a camera at home or with your attorney.

17. Good attorneys do not attack witnesses at depositions. Their goal is to find out as much as they can from the witness and smart lawyers know an aggressive approach usually does not further that goal. Do not be surprised if opposing counsel is courteous and gracious during the deposition but turns vexatious and sarcastic at trial. This is common. Similarly, the good attorney may not attempt to extract concessions from you at the deposition but may very well do so later at trial.

18. Unless this is a deposition to preserve evidence or perpetuate testimony for trial, your attorney may ask you very few ques-

tions at the deposition or none at all. The only purpose for your attorney to ask you questions would be to clarify a matter. Everything else is reserved for trial.

19. Always remain polite. "Yes, sir" or "Yes, ma'am" are appropriate responses in most parts of the country. Some attorneys will try to provoke you in order to gauge how you will respond at trial. If successful in "pushing your buttons" at the deposition, as demonstrated by your angry response, opposing counsel will probably use the same tactic at trial. Keep your composure and things will go much better.
20. When the attorneys are done questioning you, the court reporter or one of the attorneys will ask if you want to review the deposition for accuracy. Insist on it. While court reporters are generally good at their craft, a single word misunderstood by the court reporter, if transcribed inaccurately, can have serious repercussions. A copy of the transcript will then be sent to you. Review it and report any errors to your attorney before signing anything.

Section Three: How Depositions Are Used at Trial

There are two primary ways depositions are used at trial. The first is to refresh the memory of a witness. "Stage fright" or lapse of time may cause a witness to forget information sought at trial. If a witness testifies that she or he cannot remember in response to a question, a deposition may be used for assistance.

The common procedure is for the interrogating counsel to approach the witness, show the witness the relevant portion of the deposition transcript, ask the witness to read it silently, then follow with, "Does that refresh your memory?" If the witness still cannot recall the subject matter, the attorney may offer the deposition portion as evidence.

By far the more common use of a deposition at trial is to impeach a witness by demonstrating a prior inconsistent statement. Most attorneys will not allow the witness to read the pertinent excerpt of the transcript but will do so themselves. This allows the attorney to add some dramatic flair to the presentation of the testimony. If counsel allows the witness to read the portion, no rule says that the witness must use any particular inflection, speed, or cadence in reading the passage.

Chapter Six

How to Improve as a Witness

> "The whole problem with the world is that fools and fanatics are always so certain of themselves, but wiser people so full of doubts." —Bertrand Russell

> "We learn from experience. A man never wakes up his second baby just to see it smile." —Grace Williams

Ask for Constructive Criticism

If your first few times on the witness stand do not go as well as you would have liked, remember that no craft is mastered without time and effort. As with any skill, practice improves it. The more often you are deposed or testify in court, the less nerve-wracking will be the experience. But anyone who says they never get nervous when called to the witness stand is probably not being completely honest. Academy Award-winning actress Helen Hayes, then in her seventies, was asked if she got nervous on stage after her many years in theater and the movies. She responded, "I still get butterflies but I've taught them to fly in formation." Experience will help you put your anxieties in flying formation. In addition to testifying many times, there are other ways to become a peak performer.

You can reduce the learning curve if you do not let your ego get in the way. Do it by asking others for a critique of your "performance" on the stand. Likely prospects include the attorney who called you as a witness, paralegals, the jurors, and the judge. You may even solicit the opinion of opposing counsel. Anyone else in the courtroom—a clerk, court reporter, or member of the audience—can give you feedback as well.

Be sensitive to the fact that the case is not over, at a minimum, until the jury verdict is received. So don't approach a juror until then. With opposing counsel or the judge, it may be wise to wait until the time for appeal has passed and there is no chance of a retrial before asking for a critique.

Make clear to the potential critic that you are asking these questions because you sincerely want to improve your skills, that you have a thick hide and can take any criticism without hard feelings, and that you respect their opinion. What should you ask? Consider the following questions:

Did I exhibit any annoying habits or mannerisms?

How was my delivery?

Was I properly dressed?

Was there anything about my appearance that stood out in your mind?

Was I easy to understand?

Did I use good examples?

Did I appear to be well prepared?

Did I appear confident?

Did I appear to be respectful of the judge?

Was the attitude I displayed toward the opponent's attorney proper?

What suggestion would you make for me to improve as a witness?

Thank them for their time and thoughts. You do not have to change your behavior simply because one critic thinks you should. Take all of the advice, think about it carefully, then glean the best of it and put it to use. It is helpful to keep notes about tips you have learned. Before your next stint on the witness stand, read through those notes as part of your trial preparation.

If you cannot find a critic, reflect on what points were raised during cross-examination. Upon reflection, you may decide to change your standard operating procedures. Every time you testify, you should learn something that will make you a better witness.

It is axiomatic that to be perceived as trustworthy you cannot be an imposter. While certain acting skills such as projecting your voice adequately and use of body language may be a little unnatural for you at first, acquiring those skills does not change the core of your personality. In the end, you have to be yourself. By familiarizing yourself with the information in this book, you will be less anxious and more natural when you take the witness stand. You *will be* a better witness.

Don't Lose Faith

Our court trials have evolved from a time when jurors were those who lived closest to the defendant and probably had first-hand knowledge of the alleged crime, to a system where such first-hand knowledge bars jury service. In modern trials, prospective jurors who have had experience with the particular type of crime involved in the case are routinely excused. Attorneys also weed out potential jurors who have strong feelings about the case.

Next, witnesses testify before the jury. These are the people who were present when the crime was committed and have first-hand knowledge of the facts. But jurors are typically not allowed to ask these witnesses any questions. Our system assures the jury cannot ask the one question they most want to ask: "Has the defendant done anything like this before?"

When it is all over, the jury, those people selected because they knew nothing about the event, tell the people who *were* there (the witnesses), what happened; they do this by their verdict. Is it any wonder that mistakes are made and unjust verdicts occasionally returned?

As a trial judge, I made it a practice to meet with jurors after every trial, not to congratulate or criticize, but to thank them for their service and ask if they had any questions. Many trials are highly emotional events and I found jurors appreciated the opportunity to talk to an impartial person who had listened to the same evidence they had.

In the course of these meetings, when there was a "not guilty" verdict, invariably one of the jurors would tell me, "We think the defendant did it, but the prosecution just did not prove it beyond a reasonable doubt." Thereafter, what usually followed was a list of the things not proven satisfactorily, questions not answered, or witnesses not called.

You must distinguish those factors which you can influence from those beyond your control. You *can* influence the jury's opinion of your credibility. You control your appearance. You control how well you know the facts of your case. You control how you communicate these facts to the judge or jury. But you cannot control the presentation of evidence at trial. Nor can you dictate what six or twelve people do once they start deliberating in the jury room.

Do your best but recognize that you are but one cog in the machinery called justice. The system may not always turn out the right product but if you do your job well enough, there is certainly a better chance that the correct decision will be reached. Take pride in having done your part well and leave it there. In so doing, you almost certainly will prevent embarrassment on the witness stand and will enhance the view others have of you and law enforcement officers generally.

Chapter Seven

Writing and Using Arrest Reports

You may have considered skipping this chapter because it is has been drilled into you ever since your days at the academy that good report writing is essential to effective law enforcement. Just like the advice your mother gave you about not slouching and eating all your vegetables, the admonitions about report-writing are true. When it comes to testifying in court, you are at a serious disadvantage if your arrest report was not well-written.

The reason for this is simple: you experience too many events in your professional life to remember the details of each one. You may have dozens of encounters with the public during one shift. Arrests pile one on top of the other and are easily blended in your memory.

Seasoned officers recognize it is dangerous to rely on memory alone when testifying. Defense attorneys typically spend at least some time during cross-examination posing questions designed to test the memory of the witness. For example, the attorney may ask details about the clothing worn by the defendant, the weather, lighting, or road conditions at the time of arrest.

Being human, we forget things, sometimes quickly. Memory is not like a fine wine; it does not improve with age. This does not mean you cannot remember an incident that happened long ago. For example, you may not remember what you did on a particular day in August of 2001 but you may have a very good recollection of where you were and who you were with on September 11 of that year when the Twin Towers fell in New York City. The passage of time, alone, does not obliterate memories. But aside from repressed memories, time does not improve recollection either.

Your age and the time of day may impact how well you remember events. In one study subjects were asked at what time of the day they thought their ability to remember was at its peak. Most younger subjects had no preference between morning, mid-day, and evening. One study showed students did better on memory tests in the afternoon[12] but other research showed young adults performed equally well on memory tests throughout the day. Since many officers work night shifts, the research referencing specific times of day must be translated. For these officers, "morning" means within a few minutes or hours after sleeping, regardless of the time of day.

Most older subjects, 83% of them, thought they remembered better in the morning.[13] They were right. Research showed that when these older subjects were tested at the time they preferred, their scores were as high as those for young adults.

Of course, generalities are just that. Individuals may vary in their ability to remember better at different times of the day. Other factors may come into play as well. Caffeine apparently helps older people remember better when it is consumed during their off-peak hours.[14]

Some introspection on your part is worthwhile. Try to figure out when you are at your peak or, probably more importantly, when your memory is at its worst. It is that time of day when you must make extra effort to record details in your report.

No matter how good or bad your memory, a good report will help you prepare for your next appearance in court. There is an added benefit, too. Defense attorneys are often swamped with cases and must prioritize them, that is, decide which are worth taking to trial. The weak cases get plea-bargained. They "go away" so that more time can be devoted to meritorious ones.

A major factor in the defense lawyer's decision-making process involves that lawyer's perception of the prosecution's witnesses. In a DWI case, the verdict often hinges on the credibility of one person — the arresting officer. If the jury believes the officer, the defendant is usually dead in the water.

Although a DWI case can be tried to a judge without a jury, a "bench trial," this is almost never done. Judges have heard the typical defenses in DWI cases so many times they are virtually immune to arguments that some jurors find persuasive. Defense attorneys are always hoping to seat one person on the jury who has the attitude, "There but for the grace of God go I." Similarly, they are pleased when jurors become confused by the evidence and associate this with a "reasonable doubt," leading them to vote an acquittal. Judges are not so easily confused. Alternatively, the defense wants a juror who dislikes law enforcement. Sympathy for the defendant or mistrust of an officer can lead to an acquittal in a jury case much more easily than in a bench trial.

When a defense attorney reads a well-written report, the attorney envisions how the officer who wrote it will come across on the witness stand. After reading a good report, the attorney may then tell the client, "Listen, I don't see any weaknesses in this case and it looks like a long shot to win at trial. It will cost you another $1,500 if you want me to push this to trial. What do you want to do?" Often, the client decides to plead guilty. Good report writing may save you the need to testify at all.

If you are called to testify, you want your report to be detailed and accurate. This is true in every criminal case but particularly so in DWI cases because they tend to be rather mundane for experienced officers. It is easier to remember the details surrounding a homicide or crash that resulted in a death than one of a hundred DWIs the officer had.

Another reason why report writing in DWI cases must be complete and accurate is that, unlike many other criminal cases, so many of these go to trial. In several states, 15–25% of all jury trials are for DWI charges. DWI cases end up being tried to a jury for several reasons. First, the federal government has offered strong financial incentives to states which adopt minimum mandatory penalties in DWI cases. That means DWI defendants cannot expect a light sentence from a friendly judge. With mandatory sentencing, every judge is bound to give at least a minimum fine and order the defendant to complete a chemical dependency evaluation.

Secondly, although the charge of DWI is typically a misdemeanor, unlike other misdemeanors, it carries very serious consequences. Insurance rates for those convicted of DWI can double or worse. Those increased rates may stay in effect for years after the DWI event. DWI convictions carry with them the loss of driving privileges. For some people a DWI conviction means the loss of a job. For others, it is an extreme inconvenience to be without private transportation. This is particularly true in rural areas where there is little or no public transit available.

When penalties increase, the demand for jury trials does likewise. Most people will not fight a speeding ticket even if they think they are innocent because it is not worth the time and effort. But those charged with a more serious offense are very likely to deny guilt and seek a trial because the cost-to-benefit ratio dictates it. DWI cases are more akin to felonies than to misdemeanors in that the perceived penalties are so serious that defendants feel compelled to resist the charges.

The arresting officer in a DWI case should know there is a significant chance that the case will end up going to trial. If it does, the officer's report can make or break the case.

What should a good report contain? Later chapters will acquaint you with some of the favorite paths defense attorneys take during cross examination of an arresting officer. A review of those topics typically explored by defense attorneys will alert officers to the subjects which they should address in their arrest reports. Officers should also be aware that defense attorneys will question them about "omitted facts."

Here are three tips regarding report-writing and notes applicable in every DWI case.

1. Use all the senses in describing events. The five senses are sight, smell, touch, taste, and hearing, a categorization attributable to Aristotle. Police reports always include descriptions of what officers see. The next most prevalent sense employed in a typical police report is that of hearing. But the other senses—smell, touch, and taste—are rarely used to describe anything in reports. This is unfortunate because we remember better those events described to us with atten-

tion given to all of the senses. Teachers,[15] therapists working with Alzheimer patients, and memory enhancement facilitators[16] all vouch for the effectiveness of using a poly-sensory approach to learning and remembering. The more senses involved in the learning exercise, the greater the chance the subject will be accurately remembered. When an officer describes the events leading to a DWI arrest, a jury is more likely to remember the facts described if the officer uses more than the sense of sight to recreate the scene.

Here are some examples of facts which could be included in a report:

> The road or sidewalk where the driver performed the walk-and-turn test was dry and not slippery.
>
> The odor of alcoholic beverage coming from the driver's breath was sour. Substitute mildly pungent, stale, smoky, acid-smelling, rank, intense, or powerful instead of the typical descriptive words "strong," "moderate," or "slight."
>
> His face looked like someone who had been out in cold weather for a while, with his cheeks and nose a pinkish color.
>
> His speech was sluggish.
>
> He sounded as if his tongue was really thick.
>
> He tottered while he stood and I reached out to steady him because I didn't want him to get hurt.
>
> His voice sounded slushy and sloppy.

Many officers would benefit from picking up a thesaurus and looking up more descriptive words to replace the standard ones used by law enforcement.

2. Include the arrestee's words in your report by using quotation marks. You do not have to be exact but recall his language as best you can and put it in quotes. There is nothing more damning than the defendant's own words in describing his impairment. "I'm not gonna take that test 'cuz I know I can't pass it." "Just take me to jail, officer." "I didn't even see you parked there [or coming from behind me]." "It was my buddy's birthday." "C'mon, man, I was almost home."

All of these statements are admissible in court even though they are hearsay. Statements of a defendant fit into one of the long-recognized exceptions to the hearsay rule which prevents out-of-court statements from being offered in court to prove the truth of the matter asserted in the statement. If the defendant said it, you can almost always tell the jury what he said.

A caution about profanity: If the person arrested for DWI lets loose with profanity, be sure to document it in quotes. Do not water it down or clean up the language. You can use "f***" or "sh**" in your report rather than "fuck" or "shit" if you insist, but it is better to simply write it out just as you heard it.

When it comes time to testify you may be asked a question like, "What did he say to you after you asked him if he had been drinking that night?" If you know the response is going to contain profanity, turn to the judge before answering and say, "Your Honor, may I use the exact language the defendant used?" This alerts the judge and the jury that you are about to use profanity. It makes it clear that the swear words are not of your own choosing but a recitation of the defendant's words. This shows respect for the judge and the jury, which is always a good idea.

The judge will not ask you to clean up the language and will undoubtedly answer, "Yes." Then go ahead and tell the court what the defendant said. You do not have to do this in a monotone either. If the defendant said, "It's none of your f***ing business!" you can use the same tone used by the defendant when you relay his statement to the court.

3. Do not take your notes with you to the witness stand. Everyone who testifies gets nervous on the witness stand. Even seasoned veterans of the courtroom feel their blood pressure rise when their credibility is challenged. Witnesses adopt physical and mental tricks to calm their jangling nerves. Your notes fall into the former category. "I'd be lost on the witness stand without my notes!" several officers have told me. Nonsense. You do not need them. Taking them with you to the stand may actually hurt your case.

In DWI trials, the defense attorney is provided a copy of your report well before the trial. Through the process of discovery the parties can ask for copies of an opponent's reports, results of breath or blood tests, and most anything else that will help them defend the case. Defense counsel will know which witnesses will testify and they have a good idea what they will say on the witness stand.

If, during direct examination, the prosecutor asks a question and you can't remember what your notes reflect on that subject, rest assured your failing memory will not ruin the day. When a witness fails to recollect something, an attorney can "refresh memory" by using the witness's notes. The exchange often goes something like this:

Prosecutor:	In addition to the beer cans, did you notice anything else in Smith's vehicle shortly after the collision?
Officer:	I don't recall right now.
Prosecutor:	Would it refresh your memory if you could review your notes from February 13?
Officer:	Yes, it would.
Prosecutor:	Your Honor, may I approach the witness for purposes of refreshing recollection?
Judge:	Yes, you may.

(Counsel brings the officer's report to the witness stand and allows the witness to read it.)

Prosecutor:	Does that refresh your memory regarding what you saw?
Officer:	Yes it does.
Prosecutor:	What else did you notice in the vehicle?
Officer:	I also saw a cardboard box that said Budweiser on the side, the kind used to hold a twelve-pack of beer.

Any good trial lawyer will know well in advance of trial what you will say in response to any question posed. If you are not forthcoming with the anticipated answer, the attorney will find a way to bring it out.

Witnesses fear looking unintelligent when being cross-examined Many of them think the jury won't believe them if they can't remember every detail about the case. This simply is not true.

Often, the wisest words in a witness's vocabulary are "I don't know." No one expects you to have memorized voluminous material about the case. You are human and most of us do not have photographic memories. We all forget details. That is why we write reports.

If opposing counsel wants to score a point by using something you've included in one of your reports, the attorney will ask you directly about it. If you can't recall the details, the cross-examiner will use the same technique to refresh your recollection as the prosecutor did in the previous example.

There are at least two reasons not to take notes to the witness stand. First, unless you know exactly where the information can be found in the papers on your lap, it will take some time to hunt it down. This can be distracting to the jury. Worse, if you fumble for too long, you may look inept. Anything that delays the trial is viewed with disfavor by the participants, including the judge and jury. When you testify from memory, jurors are more likely to be impressed with your knowledge and competence.

Second, Rule 612 of the Rules of Evidence allows the cross-examiner to review any notes or papers you take with you to the stand. Let's assume you have some notes or reports with you on the stand, which for one reason or another, were never provided to opposing counsel during the discovery process. If you take them with you to the witness stand, and they are revealed for the first time to the cross-examining attorney, you may be subjected to some nasty questions implying you are hiding evidence to prejudice the case.

If your notes take up more than a page or two, opposing counsel may ask the judge for a recess in order to review them before continuing with your cross-examination. If the judge is so inclined, and this is more likely when the request is made close to the typical morning, lunchtime, or afternoon breaks in the trial, a recess will be granted. You do not want this to happen. It gives opposing counsel more time to develop questions aimed at discrediting your testimony. In effect, you become your own worst enemy. You should not give opposing counsel this opportunity.

So write comprehensive and detailed reports, but do not take them with you to the witness stand. Leave them in a folder on one of the benches or seats in the courtroom. Then, if you truly need them, they are readily accessible.

If you earn a reputation among defense lawyers as someone who writes good reports and testifies capably at trial, the odds of defendants pleading guilty before trial increase. If the case does go to trial, a good report will help prepare you to testify about the facts which occurred months earlier. Defense attorneys do not like cross-examining witnesses who are well-prepared. If you want to reduce the likelihood of testifying in court and win those cases which go to trial, the best way to begin is by writing good reports.

Chapter Eight

An Introduction to Field Sobriety Testing

Field sobriety testing is as old as the laws prohibiting impaired drivers from traveling our public roads. The need for such testing was nicely summarized by Dr. Marcelline Burns.[17]

> The simple fact is that within a short time a traffic officer must warn, cite, arrest, or release every motorist who is stopped. Making no decision is not an option, nor is deferring the decision to a later time. The officer must make the often difficult decision, basing it on observations of driving, the driver's general behavior, appearance, and statements, and performance of roadside tests. The goal is (or ought to be) the release of nonimpaired drivers and the arrest of DWI drivers. Given that goal, common sense dictates the use of roadside tests that have been shown in scientific studies to be the "best." Common sense also asks, "If not these best tests, then what?" It is telling in the extreme that the challengers to HGN offer no alternatives. Their argument is not, "Use Test X, which is a better test, instead of HGN." It is simply, "Do not use HGN."

A host of tests have enjoyed widespread popularity in the law enforcement community over the years. Some of the oldest, like reciting the alphabet and counting backwards, are regularly employed today. Others, like the finger-to-nose test, have fallen out of favor. These non-standardized tests will be discussed in more detail later.

An arresting officer should be aware that regardless of which field sobriety tests are performed, a defense attorney will, through cross examination, imply the wrong ones were selected by the officer.

In one recent DWI trial, the arresting officer administered the HGN, alphabet, and counting backwards tests. The officer chose not to administer the walk-and-turn or one-leg stand tests because the driver claimed to be recovering from hip surgery. The driver failed each of the tests administered by the officer. The defense attorney's closing argument to the jury went something like this:

> *Members of the jury, my client Tom is a simple man. He never got beyond high school. He doesn't read a newspaper and does not subscribe to any magazines. Many, many years ago, when he was in school, he did poorly in math. He is a man who works with his hands. While most of you good folks may not have trouble with the alphabet or counting problems, Tom is not so blessed.*
>
> *And these tests the officer gave Tom—alphabet and counting backwards tests—they don't even have an acceptable grading scheme. You heard the officer testify that there are no standards for these tests. If someone stops while counting backwards and asks the officer for clarification like "What number do you want me to stop at?" this officer rates that as a failed test.*
>
> *I don't know about you folks, but when I learned my A-B-Cs, I was taught a little song. I'll bet it's playing in your head right now because we all learned it when we were small. Well, this officer said he would rate it a failure if someone used that little song to help remember the letters in the alphabet. Yet the officer admitted there is no study that says you are necessarily drunk if you use that song to help your memory.*
>
> *And counting backwards—what kind of a test is that? When are you ever asked to do that in real life? The only time I can think of is when they are about to launch a rocket into space, and then they only count down from 10 to 1. Again, the officer had to admit there is absolutely no scientific evidence to support the theory that failing to say certain numbers BACK-*

WARDS in a particular sequence is proof of anything. This isn't science, ladies and gentlemen, this is science fiction.

What about the tests the officer could have given but deliberately chose to disregard? You heard the officer testify there is an agency, supported by your tax dollars no less, that has spent a great deal of money researching what the best, most reliable tests are. There are three of them, the HGN, walk-and-turn, and one-leg stand. I'll talk about that eye test later but what I want you to think about is this: Why did the officer select only one of the three most reliable tests to give to Tom? Was he afraid Tom would pass them? He claims Tom said something about hip surgery. Even if that was true, Tom could have used his other leg to perform the one-leg stand test. And he could still walk in a straight line. People who have had hip surgery don't lose their ability to walk straight. What was he thinking? Maybe he made up his mind that Tom was already guilty after taking that goofy eye test and didn't want to give Tom one of these other approved tests because Tom would have done well on them.

You folks get to decide whether the officer did the right thing, the fair thing, when he selected tests that Tom would have a hard time passing, and skipped the tests where Tom could have shown he was okay to drive. You get to decide if this is how you want law enforcement to operate in this county. And if you agree that this selective testing was unfair and unreliable, you should let the police know about it. You can do that—and you should do that—by finding Tom not guilty of DWI.

The jury acquitted Tom of the DWI charge. They swallowed the defense argument—hook, line, and sinker. Several of the jurors went so far as to sign a note to the police chief admonishing him for allowing his officers to use "selective tests" during field sobriety testing!

The arresting officer acted appropriately but the jury found otherwise. The point to be remembered is that an officer will be criticized by defense counsel no matter which tests or how many of them were administered. This is true regardless of how well the tests were administered by the officer.

If the same tests are given by an officer in every DWI case, the defense attorney's cross-examination may go something like this:

Attorney:	Officer, how did you select the tests you gave to my client that night?
Officer:	I like to use the same tests for everyone.
Attorney:	You mean to tell me you don't differentiate the tests given regardless of the age of driver?
Officer:	Not really, no.
Attorney:	So you would have my grandmother attempt to do the one-leg stand test?
Officer:	Well, no, probably not.
Attorney:	Do you take into consideration the driver's physical condition?
Officer:	Yes, if they had an injury or something like that.
Attorney:	What about illness and fatigue? Do you take them into consideration?
Officer:	I don't believe I have ever asked about fatigue.
Attorney:	What about weight? Would you ask someone who is very heavy to do the one-leg stand test?
Officer:	I guess it would depend. I usually ask them if there is any reason why they couldn't perform the test.
Attorney:	Do you factor in the shoes or other clothing they are wearing?
Officer:	If they are wearing boots, I ask if they prefer to do the outside tests with the boots off.
Attorney:	But that doesn't work when the weather makes the road surface too (hot or cold), does it?

Officer: Well, if the weather is bad, I don't do outside tests.

Attorney: And that would include strong winds?

Officer: Sure.

In closing argument, the attorney may argue the arresting officer was "flying by the seat of his pants," that is, selecting field sobriety tests on a whim and thereby treating people unfairly.

Another general line of attack involves the nervousness attendant to being stopped by a law enforcement officer.

Attorney: Would you agree with me that most people are nervous when stopped?

Officer: I suppose so, yes.

Attorney: Would you also agree that it is normal for people to make physical and mental mistakes when they are nervous?

Officer: That could happen.

Attorney: You have no idea what was going through my client's mind during the tests you gave him, do you?

Officer: No.

Attorney: In fact, there really is no objective way to measure the level of nervousness my client experienced that night, is there?

Officer: No.

Attorney: And you have no way to measure my client's ability to handle stress, do you?

Officer: He did not seem overly nervous or stressed to me.

Attorney: Have you ever tried to hide your nervousness from someone else?

Officer: I suppose I have.

The questioning may then turn to conditions present when the officer first took field sobriety tests so that a favorable comparison can be made to the conditions present when the client was tested.

Attorney: Where did you first get your training on field sobriety tests? At the academy?

Officer: Yes.

Attorney: And since that time you have administered those tests how many times?

Officer: Several hundred times, I suppose.

Attorney: But the first time you took the test it was in the middle of the day?

Officer: Yes.

Attorney: In a well-lit room?

Officer: Yes.

Attorney: When you were well-rested?

Officer: I can't remember back that far.

Attorney: When you were initially trained, they told you to look for signs of impairment, right?

Officer: Yes, they did.

Attorney: And they call those clues, right?

Officer: Yes.

Attorney: Sort of like the board game where you accuse Professor Plum of committing the murder with the candlestick in the conservatory?

Officer: Well, they are called clues, yes.

Attorney: So when you were in training, it was sort of like a game where you are looking for clues, signs of impairment?

Officer: I wouldn't say it was a game.

Attorney: But you were fairly relaxed when you first took a field sobriety test, isn't that true?

Officer:	I suppose so; I really don't remember.
Attorney:	Well you were not exactly stressed out about having another officer give you a field sobriety test, were you?
Officer:	Probably not.
Attorney:	And when you first took the test it was inside a building, right?
Officer:	Yes.
Attorney:	There was no traffic whizzing by?
Officer:	No.
Attorney:	And there was no police chatter on the radio when you took the test, true?
Officer:	That's right.
Attorney:	And the temperature was comfortable?
Officer:	Yes.
Attorney:	You were wearing comfortable clothing?
Officer:	Yes.
Attorney:	You didn't do as well on the tests that first time as you would now, isn't that true?
Officer:	I suppose that is true.
Attorney:	You do better with practice, right?
Officer:	Yes.

Now, the attorney will examine the conditions present at the scene of the arrest. Bear in mind, the attorney will have reviewed a video of the stop if one exists and customize the questioning consistent with what is observed on the video.

Attorney:	When did you start your shift on the day before you arrested my client?
Officer:	I started at 10:00 p.m.
Attorney:	So when you stopped my client around 1:00 a.m., that was about in the middle of your work day?

Officer: Yes.

Attorney: But it was well after my client's normal bedtime?

Officer: I guess I don't know that.

Attorney: Now I want you to describe the setting for the tests you selected. You parked your patrol car behind my client's vehicle and slightly closer to the roadway, correct?

Officer: Yes.

Attorney: You do that for safety due to passing cars and trucks?

Officer: Yes.

Attorney: Then you had my client move toward the shoulder of the road because traffic can be dangerous, right?

Officer: Yes.

Attorney: How wide was that shoulder?

Officer: About five feet.

Attorney: Was there any gravel on the shoulder?

Officer: I didn't notice.

Attorney: But traffic continued to pass by?

Officer: Yes.

Attorney: And you left your emergency lights on?

Officer: Yes.

Attorney: And your headlights were still on?

Officer: Yes.

Attorney: Were they on brights?

Officer: Yes.

Attorney: Did my client face towards or away from traffic?

Officer: He was facing toward traffic.

Attorney:	So he may have been blinded by oncoming headlights?
Officer:	I don't know about that.

If the officer says the client was facing away from traffic, the attorney may ask:

Attorney:	So he had no warning of approaching cars or trucks?
Officer:	No.
Attorney:	Would it be fair to say it was dark out but interrupted by sporadic lights from traffic?
Officer:	Yes.
Attorney:	And those sporadic lights also caused moving shadows in the area where the two of you were standing?
Officer:	Probably, yes.
Attorney:	The weather conditions that day were (windy, cold, rainy, snowing)?
Officer:	Yes.
Attorney:	Were some of the passing vehicles quite large, like semis, trucks, or motor homes?
Officer:	I did not pay close attention to that.
Attorney:	Is it possible that the air pressure or suction from those large vehicles could have been felt by my client?
Officer:	I suppose it is possible.
Attorney:	Was there chatter on your police radio during testing?
Officer:	Again, I did not pay close attention to that.
Attorney:	You are so accustomed to that noise that it probably doesn't distract you, is that fair to say?

Officer:	Yes.
Attorney:	Now all of those conditions may have ratcheted up my client's anxiety, am I right?
Officer:	They could have.
Attorney:	Did you ask my client about his stress or nervousness before administering your tests?
Officer:	No, I didn't.

The attorney may then argue to the jury that one should not expect someone like his client to perform well on tests foreign to him, especially under nerve-wracking conditions. In effect, the attorney is asking for jurors to empathize with the driver.

Unfortunately, far too many jurors have driven while impaired. Many of them do empathize, to put it mildly, with the defendant's predicament. For these jurors, it does not take a strong argument to convince them to acquit. When you combine this attitude with the strong legal presumption in favor of innocence, it is not surprising that some solid DWI arrests result in not guilty verdicts.

Chapter Nine

Horizontal Gaze Nystagmus Test

Currently, there are three field sobriety tests recommended for use by the National Highway Traffic and Safety Administration (NHTSA). They are the horizontal gaze nystagmus or HGN test, the walk-and-turn test, and the one-leg stand test. Extensive research preceded the recommendations from NHTSA with a goal of providing law enforcement with reliable tests that could be easily administered in the field. When the HGN, walk-and-turn, and one-leg stand are used together, NHTSA found they are 83% accurate in discriminating between drivers with BACs above and below 0.10%.

Of the three field sobriety tests recommended by NHTSA, the HGN has more scientific research backing up the claim of its reliability than the other two tests. It also has a higher degree of reliability than the walk-and-turn or one-leg stand tests.

The HGN test has some unique advantages over other field sobriety tests. First, the test results cannot be compromised through practice. Many drinking drivers practice walking a straight line, doing the one-leg stand and other non-standardized field sobriety tests typically used in their area. It is not uncommon for someone whose alcohol concentration level exceeded .18 to pass one or more field sobriety tests. Practice may not make perfect, but it sure helps.

The second distinct advantage of the HGN test is that it may be used with almost any subject. Unless the subject has had head trauma or some other serious medical condition affecting vision, the HGN test can be administered regardless of the subject's age or physical health. It serves as a protection to those drivers who have not consumed alcohol but for other reasons cannot perform well on balance tests. The HGN can be conducted when the savvy drinking driver mentions his "trick knee" or old football injury as a reason for failing the walk-and-turn or one-leg stand test.

A third advantage of the HGN test is that it can be performed in the officer's patrol car. When weather conditions are not conducive to testing outside, the HGN may still be administered. Defense attorneys have argued that overhead dome lights or the lack of frontal positioning during the test skewed the results but those attacks are not supported in the literature nor have the courts bought in to them.

Because the HGN test has greater reliability than most tests and one cannot practice in order to pass the test, it has come under fire from the defense bar to a greater extent than other field sobriety tests. Courts across the country have upheld the admissibility of HGN test results so long as proper foundation is laid.[18] The proper foundation for such testimony, which the prosecution may lay in the presence of the jury, includes a description of the officer's training, education, and experience in administering the test and a showing that the test was administered properly. The foundation may not include any discussion regarding the accuracy with which HGN test results correlate to, or predict, a BAC of greater or less than .10%.[19]

The HGN test is fairly easy to administer. Directions are clearly explained in the DWI Detection and Standardized Field Sobriety Testing Student Manual, February 2006 Edition, published by the U.S. Department of Transportation. It should be done in a way that ensures the subject's eyes can be seen clearly, i.e., in a well-lit area or by use of a flashlight to illuminate the subject's face, while not shining directly in the eyes. The subject should not face toward blinking lights of a police cruiser or passing cars, which may cause optokinetic nystagmus. Optokinetic nystagmus occurs when an object quickly passes through the field of vision such as when utility poles alongside a highway move through the field of vision while driving.

With the head still, the eyes follow the stimulus, jerk back quickly, and follow the stimulus again. The subject does not have to be standing but can be sitting down. The law enforcement officer informs the subject, "I am now going to check your eyes." The officer is not "testing" the subject's vision, as an ophthalmologist or optometrist would, but instead, the officer is "checking" the eyes for the physical manifestation of HGN.

Before checking the subject's eyes, the officer asks the subject to remove eyeglasses or inquires whether the subject is wearing hard or soft contact lenses. While the removal of the eyeglasses makes it easier for the officer to observe eye movement, glasses do not affect the HGN test results. Contact lenses, hard or soft, do not affect the test in any way. While hard contact lenses may pop out when the eye moves as far to the side as it will go, officers are not taught to have subjects remove contact lenses but only to note whether the subject is wearing contacts and which type on the HGN Guide.

The officer also asks the subject whether he or she has any medical impairment that would either prohibit the subject from taking the test or that would affect the test results. The officer should note on the HGN Guide any condition that prohibits the taking of the test and then move on to the remaining standard field sobriety tests. If the subject claims to have a natural nystagmus or any other condition that may affect the test result, but does not prohibit the taking of the HGN test, the officer should note the condition but still perform the test.

Officers are instructed the subject does not have to see the object clearly to perform the HGN test. The subject only has to see the object well enough to be able to follow it with his eyes. Blurry vision is not a medical condition that prohibits the subject from taking the test or performing satisfactorily.

The HGN test requires an object or stimulus for subjects to follow with their eyes, such as a pen or the tip of a penlight. Subjects use both eyes to follow the stimulus. The officer places the object approximately twelve to fifteen inches from the subject's face and slightly higher than eye level. Placing the object above eye level opens the subject's eyes further and makes their movement easier to observe.

The officer instructs the subject to follow the object with the eyes and the eyes only while the head remains still. If a subjects have difficulty keeping their head still during the test, the officer is taught to have subjects hold their own head still by pressing the palms of their hands to their cheeks or to hold their own chin. The officer should avoid holding the subject's chin or using a flashlight as a chin rest because it brings the officer into contact with the subject and compromises officer safety. The officer then asks if the subject understands all the instructions.

After positioning the object, but before conducting the test, the officer checks for signs of medical impairment. First, the officer should note whether or not the subject has resting nystagmus. This rare condition usually indicates PCP or other drug use. The officer then checks for "equal tracking" by moving the object quickly across the subject's entire field of vision to see whether the eyes follow the object simultaneously. Finally, the officer checks for equal pupil size. Lack of equal tracking or equal pupil size may indicate blindness in one eye, a glass eye, a medical disorder, or an injury. If the subject exhibits these characteristics, the officer should discontinue the HGN test. If there has been an accident and a medical disorder or injury is apparent, the officer may want to seek medical assistance for the subject.

While conducting the test, the officer looks for six "clues," three in each eye, which indicate impairment. The left eye is checked for the clue, and then the right eye. The clues are:

1. Lack of smooth pursuit. The officer moves the object slowly but steadily from the center of the subject's face towards the left ear. The left eye should smoothly follow the object, but if the eye exhibits nystagmus, the officer notes the clue. The officer then checks the right eye. Lack of smooth pursuit is observed when the eye cannot track a stimulus moving at a constant speed. Short, fast eye movements, known as saccades, try to keep the eye on the target and appear jumpy or jerky, much like a windshield wiper dragging and catching along a dry windshield.
2. Distinct nystagmus at maximum deviation. Starting again from the center of the suspect's face, the officer moves the object toward the left ear, bringing the eye as far over as possible, and holds the object there for four seconds. The officer notes the clue if there is a distinct and sustained nystagmus at this point. The officer holds the object at maximum deviation for at least four seconds to ensure that quick movement of the object did

not possibly cause the nystagmus. The officer then checks the right eye. This is also referred to as "end point" nystagmus.

3. Angle of onset of nystagmus prior to 45 degrees. The officer moves the object at a speed that would take about four seconds for the object to reach the edge of the suspect's left shoulder. The officer notes this clue if the point or angle at which the eye begins to display nystagmus is before the object reaches forty-five degrees from the center of the suspect's face. The officer then moves the object towards the suspect's right shoulder. For safety reasons, law enforcement officers usually use no apparatus to estimate the forty-five-degree angle. Generally, forty-five degrees from center is at the point where the object is in front of the tip of the subject's shoulder.

The officer also checks for vertical nystagmus. The officer checks for vertical nystagmus by raising the object several inches above the subject's eyes. Vertical nystagmus is not one of the HGN clues. However, vertical nystagmus is a good indicator of high doses of alcohol, other central nervous system depressants or inhalants, and the consumption of the drug phencyclidine (PCP). The officer should note the result and take precautions if vertical nystagmus is evident. Vertical nystagmus does not occur when the subject is looking down, regardless of impairment.

An officer following the methodology promulgated by NHTSA is often said to be following the "approved method" for administering the HGN test. At least one court has held that the results of the HGN test "are inherently unreliable" if there is a deviation from the approved method.[20]

Any officer who testifies a driver failed the HGN test, should expect vigorous cross examination about the test and the circumstances surrounding it. If the officer did not follow the "approved method," the attorney will argue the test results are invalid. In many DUI cases, probable cause for the arrest of the subject depends on the result of the HGN test. Especially in jury cases, defense attorneys often attempt to discredit HGN test results by using one these tactics:

1. Demonstrate the officer has limited knowledge about the scientific basis for the test and that there are other possible causes of nystagmus.
2. Demonstrate the officer did not follow the "approved method" for administering the test.

These questions are designed to challenge the officer's knowledge about the scientific basis for the HGN test and demonstrating other possible causes of nystagmus.

When and where were you trained to administer the HGN?

How many classroom hours were involved in the HGN training?

Did you perform the test on sober and impaired subjects in the classroom?

How many times?

How many times have you administered the test in the field?

Are you licensed to diagnose any eye conditions?

What is nystagmus?

Are you an expert on nystagmus?

How many times have you been qualified to testify as an expert on nystagmus?

(An attorney may skip these preliminary questions with an experienced officer or one who is qualified to train others to administer the HGN.)

What follows are questions that may be asked during cross-examination and some suggested responses.

Attorney:	What is caloric nystagmus?
Officer:	I don't know.
Attorney:	What is optokinetic nystagmus?
Officer:	I don't know.
Attorney:	What is epileptic nystagmus?
Officer:	I don't know.

Attorney: What is rotational nystagmus?

Officer: I don't know.

Attorney: What is fatigue nystagmus?

Officer: I don't know.

Attorney: What is physiological nystagmus?

Officer: I don't know.

Attorney: What is eye tremor?

Officer: I don't know.

(Officers are loathe to answer "I don't know" repeatedly in response to a defense attorney's questions as they believe it makes them look uninformed. However, officers are sworn to tell the truth on the witness stand. Some officers may respond by arguing, "None of that is important." This allows the attorney to respond, "Let's let the jury decide what is important." If the officer adds information to an answer, there is a risk of bringing a new issue into the trial, one that a defense attorney is happy to pursue because it distracts the jury from the basic elements of the offense. The best advice, when the answer is unknown, is to say simply, "I don't know.")

Attorney: Were you trained that some people may have naturally occurring nystagmus?

Officer: Yes.

Attorney: Was any part of your test designed to detect those people who have naturally occurring nystagmus?

Officer: Not that I am aware of.

Attorney: Is naturally occurring nystagmus a disease or medical condition?

Officer: I am not qualified to answer that question. I am not a doctor.

Attorney: Did you ask my client if he had naturally occurring nystagmus?

Officer: No, I did not.

Attorney:	Have you ever observed less than six clues when conducting the HGN?
Officer:	Of course.
Attorney:	Did you ask if my client is near-sighted or far-sighted?
Officer:	No, because it is not a vision test. (The HGN is not a vision test. An Officer asks the subject to remove eyeglasses in order to better see the subject's eyes. A subject's inability to see the stimulus clearly does not affect the presence or absence of clues indicating impairment.)
Attorney:	Just answer my question.
Officer:	It would have been a waste of your client's time and mine to ask that, so no, I didn't.
Attorney:	(Showing impatience now) I didn't ask for an explanation. The question called for a yes or no answer.
Officer:	I tried to answer your question as honestly as I could. I'm sorry. Do you want to know what I learned in my training about naturally occurring nystagmus?

A smart defense lawyer will say, "No; just answer my question." But if the lawyer says "Yes" you could respond:

Officer:	I learned that only a tiny fraction of the population has congenital nystagmus but even those few people do not exhibit nystagmus all of the time.
Attorney:	Did you ask my client if he had naturally occurring nystagmus?
Officer:	No. I asked if he had any problems with his eyes and he said "No."

Attorney:	Do you know whether naturally occurring nystagmus is considered an illness or an ailment by the medical community?
Officer:	I'm not a doctor.
Attorney:	So you don't know?
Officer:	That is correct.
Attorney:	Was any part of your test designed to detect those people who have naturally occurring nystagmus?
Officer:	No.
Attorney:	Did you ask my client if he has ever had any head injuries?
Officer:	Yes.
Attorney:	You know that head injuries can cause nystagmus?
Officer:	Yes.
Attorney:	That is why you are trained to ask subjects about head injuries before you conduct the test?
Officer:	I suppose so, yes.
Attorney:	You were trained that people who have had head injuries should not be given the HGN test, weren't you? (If there was a collision or if the driver's vehicle left the road, expect several more questions about medical injuries and how they may have impacted the HGN test results. They will usually be couched in language about your training, i.e., "Didn't they teach you that…?" The best response is the truth: "They did not teach us what effect any particular injury would have on the test.")

Attorney:	What drugs can cause people to exhibit nystagmus?
Officer:	I am not sure.
Attorney:	Were you not trained that a whole host of drugs can cause nystagmus?
Officer:	No.
Attorney:	Did you ask my client if he consumed antihistamines that day?
Officer:	No.
Attorney:	What about caffeine?
Officer:	No.
Attorney:	Are you aware that overhead lights can cause nystagmus?
Officer:	No.
Attorney:	Have you been trained that inner ear problems can cause nystagmus?
Officer:	No.
Attorney:	And that certain eye conditions can affect the test?
Officer:	No.
Attorney:	Are you aware that traffic going by in the near vicinity can cause nystagmus?
Officer:	I was not aware of that.
Attorney:	Did you ask my client if he had any inner ear problems?
Officer:	I did not.
Attorney:	Weren't you taught there are at least 39 causes of nystagmus that having nothing to do with alcohol consumption?
Officer:	No one has ever told me that, although some defense attorneys have implied it.

Attorney:	What did you do to rule out those other causes?
Officer:	Nothing.
Attorney:	Do you really believe this is a fair test?
Officer:	I don't pass judgment on tests; I simply try to do them the way I was trained.
Attorney:	When you were trained to conduct the HGN test, were any of your instructors licensed ophthalmologists? Optometrists? Physicians? Physician assistants? Did your instructors have any medical training at all?
Officer:	No.
Attorney:	In fact, they were other law enforcement officers, isn't that true?
Officer:	Yes, they were.

These questions are designed to show the officer did not follow the "approved method" for administering the test or that the officer's memory of the event is unreliable. The first few questions establish the basis for the defense attorney's closing argument when the jurors will be told to disregard the HGN test results because the officer admitted that his failure to follow the approved method for administering the test could impact the test results.

Attorney:	When you were trained to administer the HGN test, you were taught to follow certain guidelines, correct?
Officer:	Yes.
Attorney:	Those guidelines came from the National Highway and Traffic Safety Administration, didn't they?
Officer:	Yes.
Attorney:	I'll refer to that as Nitsa for short, okay? Nitsa is the recognized authority on the administration of the HGN test, right?

Officer:	I suppose so, yes.
Attorney:	You were taught that following the guidelines is important for the results to be reliable, weren't you?
Officer:	Yes.
Attorney:	And you were taught that if you fail to follow the guidelines, the results can be compromised, correct?
Officer:	Yes.
Attorney:	When did you complete this training? (The attorney may later argue that your training was so long ago that you are not aware of recent advances in the field or that your training was so recent that you are a novice who cannot be trusted.)
Attorney:	How many times have you administered the HGN test?
Officer:	Seventy.
Attorney:	What was the first thing you did when you gave the HGN test to my client?

(If you fail to mention that you asked about eye problems or head injuries, counsel will point out how important it was that you skipped this step.)

Attorney:	Weren't you taught that people with head injuries might be unable to satisfactorily complete the test?
Officer:	Yes.
Attorney:	You wouldn't try to give this test to someone who was knocked unconscious in a vehicle accident, would you?
Officer:	Probably not.
Attorney:	In fact, you were taught this was the first important piece of information you

	should get before proceeding with the test, weren't you?
Officer:	I don't recall.
Attorney:	Yet you ignored that training, didn't you?
Officer:	I do not agree with that.

(Assuming you asked about eye problems and head injuries, questioning will turn to the procedure you followed in administering the test. Questions may be open ended, i.e., "What did you do next?" This type of question is designed to see if you leave out any important step in the process. Alternatively, you may be asked very specific questions. For example ...)

Attorney:	What is the first thing you did as part of the HGN test?
Officer:	I checked for resting nystagmus, equal pupil size, and equal tracking.

(If you omit any of the steps in the "approved method" you can be sure the defense attorney will introduce a copy of the NHTSA training manual into evidence as an exhibit, then argue to the jury that the test results are invalid because you failed to follow the "approved method.")

Attorney:	I do not see any mention that you checked for resting nystagmus in your report.
Officer:	I did not include that.
Attorney:	Nor do I see any mention of the fact that you checked for equal pupil size.
Officer:	I always do that.
Attorney:	But it is not in your report, is it?
Officer:	No.
Attorney:	And I do not see any reference to you checking for equal tracking in your report.
Officer:	That is correct, but I did it.

Attorney: It is important to do those three things because they are all part of the approved method, right?

Officer: Yes.

Attorney: You were trained to do all three of them, weren't you?

Officer: Yes.

Attorney: Although you were trained to do them, you did not think it was important to mention them in your report?

Officer: Those are not clues.

Attorney: But they are part of the standardized procedure, correct?

Officer: If I saw resting nystagmus, I would have put it in my report.

Attorney: So when you conduct a horizontal gaze nystagmus test, this is all you write, and I quote from your report: "I administered the horizontal gaze nystagmus test to Johnson. He showed six of six clues. I deemed this test a fail." That's all you did?

Officer: Yes.

Attorney: Isn't it part of your training and highly recommended, that you take field notes on the HGN test?

Officer: Some people do.

Attorney: But the training says you're supposed to do it, right?

Officer: You can. It almost comes down to an officer's safety. Who is going to have a pen and pad in their hand when they're doing some of this stuff?

Attorney:	I'm going to quote from Roman Numeral VIII, number 14 of the NHTSA training manual: "For the purposes of the arrest report and your testimony, it is not enough to record the total number of clues on three tests. It helps determine whether there is probable cause to arrest, but to secure a conviction more descriptive evidence is needed." And then they recommend doing field notes, correct?
Officer:	If that is what it says, then that is part of the training.
Attorney:	So you did not follow your training when you gave the HGN test to my client, right?
Officer:	In that small aspect, no.
Attorney:	Which eye did you test first?
Officer:	The left eye.
Attorney:	To your left, or his left eye?
Officer:	His left eye.
Attorney:	What did you use for a stimulus or stylus?
Officer:	I used my index finger.
Attorney:	Where did you position the stimulus at the start of the test?
Officer:	I started with my finger 12–15" directly in front of your client's face, slightly above eye level.
Attorney:	How many seconds did you take to move the stimulus out to the right?
Officer:	For lack of smooth pursuit, about two seconds.
Attorney	How long did you hold the stimulus at 45 degrees?

Officer:	For onset of nystagmus at 45 degrees, I held it long enough to see if there was any nystagmus, perhaps a couple of seconds, then moved back toward the center and to the other eye.
Attorney:	What did you use to measure 45 degrees?
Officer:	I took it out to the end of my shoulder which is about 45 degrees.
Attorney:	Did you use any device to set 45 degrees to determine the onset of nystagmus?
Officer:	No.
Attorney:	So your estimate of 45 degrees is just that, an estimate or guess?
Officer:	No.
Attorney:	This wasn't exactly a precise test, was it?
Officer:	I don't know what you mean by that.
Attorney:	How did you determine how far to move the stimulus when you tested for nystagmus at maximum deviation?
Officer:	I moved it out to a point where I could see very little or no white in the corner of his eye.
Attorney:	Did you ask my client if he could see the stimulus when it was at maximum deviation?
Officer:	No.
Attorney:	So you cannot be certain that he could actually see the stimulus, true?
Officer:	The point is not whether he can see the stimulus but the direction his eyes were looking.

Attorney: Are you aware that you can induce nystagmus by going out too far?

Officer: No, I do not recall that.

Attorney: Were you taught that there will be some nystagmus at maximum deviation even among people who have not consumed alcohol?

Officer: Again, I do not recall that.

Attorney: How many seconds did it take you to test for nystagmus at maximum deviation?

Officer: About 15 seconds.

Attorney: How long did you hold the stimulus at maximum deviation?

Officer: Four seconds for each eye.

(If the answer is any time period less than four seconds, this contradicts NHTSA guidelines and will be subject of considerable focus and criticism.)

Attorney: Did you conduct one or two passes for each part of the test?

Officer: I do two passes on each eye for each part of the test.

Attorney: If you noted a clue when you did one pass but did not observe it when you did the other pass, do you still count that as a clue?

Officer: No.

Attorney: What color are my client's eyes?

Officer: Brown.

Attorney: Where did you conduct the HGN test?

(If the test was conducted outside, the attorney may ask the following questions.)

Were your overhead strobe lights flashing at the time you conducted the test?

Was my client standing in a place where your/his headlights shined on him during the test?

Was there any traffic in the area while you conducted the HGN?

So headlights from that traffic could have shined into my client's eyes during the test?

Did you use a flashlight so you could see my client's eyes during the tests?

Where was the flashlight pointed?

Was it windy outside?

Was there any dust or pollen in the air at the time the test was given?

(If the test was conducted inside, the attorney may ask the following questions.)

Was your bright dome light in the squad car illuminated during the test?

Were there other lights coming from any instruments or radio that was between you and my client during the test?

Was your computer screen on?

How were you facing my client during the HGN?

There is a center console in your squad car, true?

So he had to twist his body to look at you?

Would it be fair to say that one of his shoulders was closer to you than the other when you conducted the test?

Attorney: Weren't you taught that you and the person tested should be looking straight at each other?

Officer: I was taught the person should be looking straight at the stimulus and I should be positioned to see both eyes.

Attorney:	In fact, according to the NHTSA manual, aren't you and the subject supposed to be standing during the HGN test?
Officer:	I was taught the subject should have his feet together, arms at the side, and look directly at the stimulus.
Attorney:	How many degrees per second did you move your stimulus?
Officer:	I do not know.

Chapter Ten

Other Field Sobriety Tests

Most law enforcement agencies and the National Highway Traffic and Safety Administration recommend three tests be administered to determine driver impairment. They are the HGN, walk-and-turn, and one-leg stand tests. These are commonly referred to as "standardized tests" because there are standardized methodologies for administering them. Theoretically, the tests are administered and scored in the same fashion nation-wide. NHTSA recommends that all three of the standardized tests be given to a suspect.

The walk-and-turn test involves a subject taking nine steps, heel-to-toe, pivoting, then taking a second series of nine steps to the starting position. There are eight possible clues indicative of impairment on this test. They are:

1. Failing to maintain balance while listening to instructions.
2. Starting too soon.
3. Stopping while walking.
4. Failing to touch heel to toe on each step.
5. Stepping off line.
6. Using arms for balance by raising them 6" or more from the sides.
7. Making an improper turn.
8. Taking an incorrect number of steps.

The one-leg stand test requires a subject to hold one leg off the ground for several seconds while counting out loud. There are four clues for this test:

1. Swaying while balancing.

2. Using arms for balance.
3. Hopping.
4. Putting the foot down.

A subject who exhibits two or more clues on either test is often said to have "failed" the test. Officers may want to avoid testifying that a subject "failed" the test but rather say that a driver exhibited signs of impairment. This undermines efforts of defense attorneys to characterize the test as an academic exercise where one can "pass" the test while getting some individual answers wrong. See the example of cross-examination on the alphabet test below. The walk-and-turn and one-leg stand tests are not academic tests.

As is true for the HGN, an officer must be thoroughly familiar with and meticulously follow the guidelines from NHTSA regarding administration of them.

For example, NHTSA recommends that these standardized tests be conducted on a reasonably dry, hard, level, non-slippery surface. This recommendation forms the basis for a host of questions from defense counsel. The following list of questions is not exclusive but illustrates how an attorney lays foundation for a later attack on the test results.

Where, exactly, on the roadway was the test conducted?

Was my client standing on the shoulder of the road or on the roadway itself?

Was there any loose gravel there?

Was there any mud or snow there?

Was the surface asphalt or concrete?

Was the roadway, like most, sloped so that moisture drains from the middle of the road toward the ditches?

Were there any cracks in the surface of the roadway?

Was the site on or near a hill or elevation in the surface?

Defense counsel may also question an officer about the weather conditions, especially if it was windy, raining, or snowing, as this could impact the test results. An attorney may ask if there was heavy traffic on the road, if large trucks went by during the testing, and later argue the vacuum created by such traffic affected a subject's balance. A sample of cross-examination on the walk-and-turn and one-leg stand tests appears at the end of this chapter.

When the standardized tests are not given, or if less than all three tests are administered, the attorney may question why this happened. There are several legitimate reasons for not giving all three standardized tests. The most common reasons for not giving the HGN test are:

a. The subject was involved in a collision and sustained a head injury.

b. The subject has an eye condition or disease.

c. The subject would not follow directions during the test.

The most common reasons for not giving the walk-and-turn or one-leg stand tests include:

a. The subject had surgery on a foot, ankle, knee, or hip.

b. The subject claimed injury to a foot, ankle, knee, or hip.

c. The subject is morbidly obese.

d. The subject exhibited such poor balance before the test that the officer deemed it unsafe to proceed with the test.

e. The surface of the roadway or area for testing was pitched, slippery, or graveled.

f. Weather conditions prohibited outside testing.

When an officer does not administer all three standardized tests, it is common for that officer to give a subject one or more non-standardized tests to determine if a subject is impaired by the consumption of alcohol or other drugs. Some of the commonly used non-standardized tests are the alphabet, partial alphabet, counting backwards, finger dexterity, and finger-to-nose tests.

Perhaps the most common of the non-standardized tests is the alphabet or partial alphabet test. The arresting officer usually inquires of the subject's educational background and whether the subject is familiar with the ABCs. If the subject responds affirmatively to the last question, the officer asks the subject to say the alphabet from A to Z without singing. Alternatively, or after the full alphabet test is administered, the officer may ask the subject to recite only a portion of the alphabet, e.g., "Begin with the letter D and continue through the letter Q."

Cross-examination may follow these lines:

Attorney: So you did not give the three tests approved by the National Highway Traffic and Safety Administration?

Officer: No, I did not.

Attorney: Instead, you gave my client a different test?

Officer: That's right.

Attorney: What do you call this test you came up with?

Officer: It is called the alphabet test.

Attorney: How did you conduct the test?

Officer: I first asked Mr. Jones if he knew his ABCs. When he said that he did, I asked him to say the alphabet from A to Z without singing.

Attorney: Where did you learn to administer this test?

Officer: At the law enforcement training academy.

Attorney: Weren't you taught that you should not include the full alphabet but rather select a part of the alphabet?

Officer: I was taught I could use the full alphabet or any part of it.

Attorney: Now this is not a standardized test, is it?

Officer: No, it is not.

Attorney: Do all other officers grade it the same way?

Officer:	I am not sure about that.
Attorney:	You don't know?
Officer:	I guess not, no.
Attorney:	How many letters wrong would you consider a fail?
Officer:	I don't grade it pass or fail. I just make note of their performance on the test.
Attorney:	So if this was the only test you gave someone and they messed up once on the test, would you arrest them for DUI?
Officer:	No, I would not.
Attorney:	How about if they had three mistakes?
Officer:	It would depend on all of the circumstances at the time.
Attorney:	So if they have errors, it might lead to an arrest and it might not; is that what you're saying?
Officer:	I suppose so.
Attorney:	When you were in school, on a 25-question test, how many wrong answers resulted in a fail?
Officer:	I don't understand what you mean.
Attorney:	Let's say you were taking a history test in school and the test had 25 questions. How many could you get wrong and still pass the test?
Officer:	I imagine that would depend on the teacher.
Attorney:	But isn't 75% typically a passing grade?
Officer:	Oh, I see what you mean. Yes, in most classes 75% would probably get you a D.

Attorney:	In my client's case, you determined that he did not do very well, correct?
Officer:	He had several errors, yes.
Attorney:	Did you give him a second chance to take the test?
Officer:	No, I did not.
Attorney:	So, apparently, you had already determined that he was under the influence, and you were going to arrest him?
Officer:	I would not say that.
Attorney:	But you did not give him another opportunity to take that test, did you?
Officer:	No.
Attorney:	Would you agree that "V" sounds like "Z"?
Officer:	I suppose to some people, it does.
Attorney:	Did you ever ask my client if he had any hearing problems?
Officer:	No, but he seemed to understand what I was saying.
Attorney:	You assume he understood because he did not say anything to the contrary, isn't that true?
Officer:	I suppose so.
Attorney:	Have there ever been times in your life when you did not understand something but you were too embarrassed or shy to ask for clarification?
Officer:	Sure.
Attorney:	Do you have any idea how many million people in this country suffer from tinnitus?
Officer:	No, I do not.

Attorney: Did you ask my client if he suffered from tinnitus?

Officer: No, I did not.

Here are some sample of cross-examination on the walk-and-turn and one-leg-stand tests. Included are sample responses an officer might give to some of the questions from defense counsel.

Cross Exam—One-Leg Stand Test

What are the clues on the one-leg stand test? *They are raising your arms for balance, putting your foot down, hopping, and swaying.*

How long do you make them hold their leg in the air? *I tell them to count out loud until I tell them to stop. I stop them if they exhibit two clues. If no clues are observed, I stop the test when the subject counts to 30.*

Did my client complete the entire one-leg stand test?

Based on your training, is the one-leg stand test more or less accurate than the HGN test?

Do you know whether it is more or less accurate for predicting impairment than the walk-and-turn test?

Did she sway during the whole test or only during a portion of it?

If she put her foot down more than once, that is still only one clue, correct?

How far did she lift her arms? *At least 6" from her side.*

Did she raise both of her arms or only one?

Isn't it true that NHTSA's approved method allows someone to raise their arms during the test without that counting as a clue?

How did you measure if her arms were raised more than 12"?

Was there any wind that night? (If you do not remember and your report does not say so, be careful not to assume it was calm. An attorney may have a weather report handy to impeach you if your testimony differs from that report.)

Did my client tell you about her bad hip? (the questioner may substitute ankle, knee, or foot) *I asked her if she had any physical condition that would make it difficult for her to do the test and she said "No."*

Have you ever had a medical problem that you would be uncomfortable talking about with a stranger?

How old are you? (At this point, counsel may glance over to an elderly juror or the judge and make a side comment like, "Just wait, your time will come." Some judges discount the results of the one-leg stand and walk-and-turn tests when conducted on subjects over 50 years of age, especially those who are overweight.)

You had never met my client before that night, had you?

If someone had a bad hip, it could affect the way they performed on the test, couldn't it?

Did you tell my client to do this test with her eyes closed?

Did you check to see if her eyes were closed during the test?

Cross Exam—Walk-and-Turn Test

Do you recall from your training how accurate the walk-and-turn test is?

When were you trained to conduct the walk-and-turn test?

Have you had any refresher courses since then?

Name the clues on that test.

Where did you conduct this test?

What kind of surface is there?

Was there any gravel on the surface?

Did you use a real line or an imaginary one?

Don't most highways have a grade or incline to allow water to run off?

Wasn't there an incline where you had my client take this test?

What kind of footwear was my client wearing that night?

Was there any overhead lighting in the area?

Were your flashing overhead lights on while my client took this test?

Did you explain the walk-and-turn test?

Did you demonstrate it? All of the test or only part?

Did you demonstrate the turn?

What is a pivot? Do you think that is a commonly understood term?

Did you inquire about any knee injury my client had?

Did you ask my client if he had any inner ear problems?

(If the test is conducted on a sidewalk, an attorney may ask questions about this.)

Did my client walk over to the sidewalk where you conducted the test?

Did she have any balance problems walking to that location?

Did she have to step up and over a curb to get there?

She didn't have any trouble with that, did she?

How many times did she miss heel-to-toe?

If she missed heel-to-toe on the first nine steps and again on the second nine steps, do you count that as one clue or two clues?

You administered this test according to the standards adopted by NHTSA, didn't you?

The method approved by NHTSA doesn't require that a person actually touch heel to toe, does it?

Did she take the wrong number of steps on the way out and on the way back, or only on half of the test?

How many steps did she take?

You say she did not perform the turn as instructed. Did she lose her balance when she made the turn?

Did you notice anything unusual about my client's walk or gait?

There's nothing in your report indicating that, either, is there?

Chapter Eleven

Arrest in the DWI Case

In criminal law there are varying standards of proof. At trial in a criminal case, the prosecution has the burden of proving the defendant committed the offense beyond a reasonable doubt. It is improper to use a percentage analogy in criminal cases. A prosecutor cannot tell a jury, "If you believe 90% of the evidence shows the defendant committed the offense, you should convict the defendant." In fact, appellate courts have reversed convictions solely on the basis of a prosecutor's argument during which percentages were mentioned, reasoning that the concept of reasonable doubt is not a mathematical one.

The burden of proof is less onerous in a civil case. For example, if an officer is sued because the officer allegedly used unreasonable force when making an arrest, the person bringing the suit, has the burden of proving the officer was at fault by a preponderance of the evidence. In layman's terms, this means the plaintiff must prove it was more likely than not that the officer used unreasonable force. In other words, if the person bringing the suit has enough evidence to convince a jury that 51% of the evidence shows fault, that is enough for that plaintiff to win the lawsuit. Obviously, the burden of proof is easier to meet in a civil case than it is in a criminal one. *Commonwealth v. Mack*, 423 Mass. 288, 291 (1996).

This brings us to the two standards of proof officers consider every day on the job: reasonable suspicion and probable cause. An officer has reasonable suspicion of something when his belief is not merely a hunch or guess but is based on facts which the officer can articulate or say.

Reasonable suspicion is the lowest rung on the burden of proof ladder. Proof beyond a reasonable doubt is the highest rung on that ladder. The second rung from the bottom is probable cause. In some states, "probable cause" has been defined as "reasonable cause" or "reasonable grounds" but the standard is the same.

The United States Supreme Court has consistently ruled that an officer may arrest a person if the officer has probable cause to believe a person has committed a crime. Probable cause exists where the facts and circumstances within the officer's knowledge and of which he had reasonably trustworthy information are sufficient in themselves to warrant a man of reasonable caution in the belief that an offense has been or is being committed. *Carroll v. United States*, 267 U.S. 132 (1925).

"These long prevailing standards seek to safeguard citizens from rash and unreasonable interferences with privacy and from unfounded charges of crime. They also seek to give fair leeway for enforcing the law in the community's protection. Because many situations which confront officers in the course of executing their duties are more or less ambiguous, room must be allowed for some mistakes on their part. But the mistakes must be those of reasonable men, acting on facts leading sensibly to their conclusions of probability. The rule of probable cause is a practical, nontechnical conception affording the best compromise that has been found for accommodating these often opposing interests. Requiring more would unduly hamper law enforcement. To allow less would be to leave law abiding citizens at the mercy of the officers' whim or caprice." *Brinegar v. United States*, 338 U.S. 160 (1949).

In court, defense attorneys frequently argue their client was illegally arrested. By that they mean the arrest was not supported by probable cause. If the argument is accepted by the court, the case is dismissed. To add insult to injury, the arresting officer may be sued for false imprisonment or violation of the arrestee's civil rights. The bottom line for the arresting officer is simple—have your ducks in a row before uttering those fateful words, "You are under arrest."

Those four words, "You are under arrest," are not magic words insofar as constitutional protections are concerned. If a person reasonably believes he is not free to leave, he is in custody for constitutional purposes. Even though the officer has not told him he is under arrest, this person may have the constitutional right to consult with an attorney before answering questions because he is in custody.

However, those four words *are* magic in the sense that many states require they be given for purposes of administrative penalties in DWI cases. These states requires that an officer tell the driver he or she is under arrest for driving or being in actual physical control of a vehicle while under the influence of intoxicating liquor. Failure to do so deprives the state of authority to suspend driving privileges.

Sometimes, the person arrested has committed a host of offenses. Consider this scenario: A law enforcement officer sees a purple-colored sedan disregard a stop sign. The officer turns on the squad car's red flashing light to stop the sedan. The sedan leads the officer on a high speed chase. Soon, the sedan crashes into another car. The driver takes off on foot. The officer eventually corners the driver in a fenced yard where the driver is combative, spits at the officer, and kicks the officer before being taken down. The driver reeks of alcohol, has slurred speech, bloodshot eyes, and sways as he stands. The officer's adrenaline level is understandably high.

In this scenario, it is easy to understand why an officer might not think of telling the driver he is under arrest for DWI when other offenses come to mind such as Reckless Endangerment, Fleeing an Officer, and Assault on a Peace Officer. These latter offenses may be felonies where DWI is typically a misdemeanor. But if the officer fails to use the magic words, the driver may escape the administrative penalty of suspended driving privileges. Perhaps, in the overall scheme of things, this is not a major problem but drivers should at least face the possibility of losing their driving privileges for their poor decisions.

It is impossible to set out the precise facts which constitute probable cause for a DWI or APC arrest. However, in order to convict anyone of DWI or APC, the prosecution must prove the driver was impaired by the consumption of alcohol. Accordingly, a defense attorney will attack an officer's conclusion that a particular observation was actually an indicator of impairment.

Alternative Explanations for Signs of Impairment

Every attorney experienced in the area of DWI law has a list of ready excuses or alternative explanations for the signs of impairment exhibited by the client. Some of them are more plausible than others. What follows are questions an officer might expect with regard to these indicia of impairment noted in reports filed by law enforcement officers.

1. Speeding
2. Bloodshot eyes
3. Watery or glossy eyes
4. Slurred speech
5. Admission to drinking
6. Fumbling with wallet or purse
7. Odor of alcoholic beverage

Speeding

Attorney:	When you were trained to use radar, did your instructor also train you to estimate speed visually and then check your visual estimate against the radar reading?
Officer:	Yes, that was part of my training.
Attorney:	I assume that after you had been on the job for a while, you became fairly good at estimating speed visually.
Officer:	I would like to think so, yes.
Attorney:	When you first saw my client's vehicle, did you estimate his speed visually before using your radar?
Officer:	Yes.
Attorney:	What speed did you estimate he was traveling?

Officer:	I estimated he was going about 65 mph.
Attorney:	How many feet were you from his vehicle when you visually estimated its speed?
Officer:	I would say about 500 feet.
Attorney:	How many feet were you from his vehicle when you first took the radar (or laser) reading?
Officer:	About 300 feet.
Attorney:	How many seconds elapsed between these two events?
Officer:	Not long.
Attorney:	Five seconds?
Officer:	No, less than that.
Attorney:	Three seconds?
Officer:	That sounds about right.

(In closing argument, the attorney can argue: "Officer Johnson is really saying my client drove 200 feet (500 feet minus 300 feet) in 3 seconds, or 67 feet per second. To convert feet per second to miles per hour, divide by 1.47. So, 67 feet divided by 1.47 equals 45 miles per hour. Using pretty simple math, the officer's own testimony shows my client was really doing 45 mph, well within the 50 mph speed limit." Officers must be aware of this tactic and be very careful in answering questions involving distance or time. If unsure of exact times or measurements, an officer should give him/herself ample leeway, e.g., "I suppose he traveled 200–300 feet in those few seconds." If you don't know the precise answer, don't pretend that you do.)

If this tactic does not work, attorneys have other lines of attack. One of them involves the accuracy of the machine used to gauge speed.

Attorney:	What kind of machine did you use to measure speed in this case?
Officer:	I used my Stalker Dual radar.
Attorney:	How do you check to see if the machine is functioning properly?

Officer:	I do a tuning fork check at the beginning and end of each shift and the machine does an internal calibration after each use.
Attorney:	At what times before and after you wrote the defendant's citation did you use the radar unit's internal calibration function?
Officer:	I do not keep track of the exact times.
Attorney:	At what times before and after you wrote the defendant's citation did you use an external tuning fork for calibration?
Officer:	I do not know the exact times, but my shift began at 5:00 p.m.
Attorney:	In your opinion, what is the difference between the internal calibration and the tuning fork calibration methods?
Officer:	I really am not qualified to answer that.
Attorney:	Do you believe that one calibration method is more accurate than the other?
Officer:	I do not know.
Attorney:	Has your radar device ever given a false reading?
Officer:	Not to my knowledge, no.
Attorney:	Isn't it true that the accuracy of a reading may be affected by the amount of traffic in the area, RFI, and the weather, among other things?
Officer:	I suppose it could.
Attorney:	Explain RFI to the jury.
Officer:	It is interference from radio frequencies.
Attorney:	Radio frequencies could come from truckers who are on their CB radios?
Officer:	I suppose that is true.

Attorney:	Were there any trucks in the area when you clocked my client on radar?
Officer:	I do not recall specifically.

Bloodshot Eyes

Attorney:	You state he had bloodshot eyes.
Officer:	Yes.
Attorney:	Did you ask what my client had been doing that day?
Officer:	No. I think I asked him where he was coming from but that's about it.
Attorney:	So you don't know whether he had spent a lot of time outdoors that day?
Officer:	No, I don't.
Attorney:	Do your eyes sometimes get red when you have been up for 20 hours?
Officer:	I don't know. Maybe they do.
Attorney:	Are you aware that many irritants can cause bloodshot eyes?
Officer:	Yes.
Attorney:	For example, some people are allergic to the dust particles and other things floating in the air?
Officer:	I suppose they are, yes.
Attorney:	Wasn't it kind of a windy day when you arrested my client?
Officer:	I do not recall it being especially windy.
Attorney:	And some people's eyes are sensitive to cigarette smoke?
Officer:	I imagine some are, yes.
Attorney:	Did you ask my client if he had any allergies?

Officer:	No.
Attorney:	Did you ask him if he had been around cigarette smoke that evening?
Officer:	No.
Attorney:	Are you aware that web sites which describe possible causes for the symptom of red eyes includes dozens of causes but not one of them is alcohol consumption? Were you aware of that?
Officer:	No.

Watery or Glossy Eyes

Attorney:	Would you agree that the environment can cause someone's eyes to water?
Officer:	Yes, I would.
Attorney:	Would you agree that a person's medical condition could cause his eyes to water?
Officer:	I suppose that is true.
Attorney:	Did you ask my client if had any medical condition that might cause his eyes to water?
Officer:	I think I asked him if he had any head injury or medical condition that affected his eyes and he said, "No."
Attorney:	That was not my question. Did you specifically ask him about any medical condition he had that may have caused glossy or watery eyes?
Officer:	No.

Slurred Speech

Attorney:	Had you ever talked to my client before the night of his arrest?

Officer: No, I never met him before that night.

Attorney: So you don't know how he normally talks, do you?

(It really perturbs an attorney to get a response like this one: "I didn't talk to him before that night, but I talked with him in the hallway today and his speech was clear as a bell." Attorneys sometimes forget to tell their client not to talk to you before or during the trial. No law prohibits such contact so long as you do not discuss the case.)

Attorney: Were you still able to understand him?

Officer: Yes.

Attorney Was every word slurred, or only a few? (Notice how the attorney gives you a limited choice—all words or only a few. In truth, many words may have been slurred, though not all.)

Officer: Some of his speech was slurred but not all of it.

Admission to Drinking

Attorney: You indicated he told you he had two or three drinks?

Officer: Yes.

Attorney: Was that something he just blurted out or was it in response to a question from you?

Officer: I asked him how much he had to drink.

Attorney: And that is just how you asked the question?

Officer: Yes.

Attorney: So you did not ask him how many alcoholic beverages he consumed?

Officer: No, but I think he knew I was talking about alcoholic drinks.

Attorney:	You assumed, but you did not ask, correct?
Officer:	Yes, that's correct.

Do you make room for the possibility that (sign of impairment) was due to (excuse)?

Fumbling with Wallet

Attorney:	You said he fumbled with his wallet. Would you admit that getting stopped by an officer can be a frightening experience?
Officer:	I suppose to some people it can be.
Attorney:	Were you in uniform?
Officer:	Yes.
Attorney:	Were your emergency lights flashing?
Officer:	Yes.
Attorney:	You were wearing a badge?
Officer:	Yes.
Attorney:	You had a firearm visible on your person?
Officer:	Yes.
Attorney:	That could make someone nervous enough to fumble with a wallet, couldn't it?
Officer:	It is possible.
Attorney:	Have you ever been arrested? (The prosecutor will probably object and you will not have to answer the question. Nevertheless, the point is made with the jury that you are unable to empathize with a normal citizen stopped by a law enforcement officer.)

Odor of Alcoholic Beverages

Attorney:	You state in your report that you detected the odor of alcoholic beverages coming from my client's vehicle, is that correct?
Officer:	Yes, I did.
Attorney:	But your report does not say that you smelled any odor of alcohol coming directly from my client. Would that be fair?
Officer:	Yes.
Attorney:	What did it smell like?
Officer:	It smelled like alcoholic beverages.
Attorney:	Well, did it smell sweet or sour?
Officer:	It just smelled like alcoholic beverages.
Attorney:	You understand, don't you, that alcohol has no odor?
Officer:	I am aware of that, yes.
Attorney:	So what you are really smelling is the soda or other fluid, not the alcohol, correct?
Officer:	It is a mixture of the two and what happens to it after it has been consumed.
Attorney:	Would it be fair to say that you cannot tell how much alcohol one has consumed by the odor alone?
Officer:	Not exactly. I mean, you cannot tell exactly how much they've had to drink but you can get an idea of how much.
Attorney:	So you are telling us that you can tell if someone has had, for example, four drinks instead of two?
Officer:	I didn't say that.
Attorney:	Can you tell, from the odor alone, whether someone has consumed four drinks as opposed to two drinks?

Officer: Probably not, no.

Attorney: Can you tell, from the odor alone, whether someone has consumed five drinks as opposed to two drinks?

Officer: I don't know if I could.

Attorney: How about six drinks rather than two?

Officer: I am not certain.

Attorney: Were you trained to tell how many drinks someone consumed based on odor alone?

Officer: No.

Attorney: So if you were asked whether someone was over the legal limit based on their odor, you would have to admit that you cannot do that, true?

Officer: I suppose so, yes.

Another tactic used to imply there was not probable cause for the arrest is to question an officer about facts that are NOT in the arrest report.

Cross-Examination on Omitted Facts

When you were first trained to be a law enforcement officer, you were taught to write arrest reports, weren't you?

And you were taught how important it was to be accurate and complete in writing those reports, correct?

And one of the reasons for writing accurate, complete reports is that it can assist you if a case later goes to trial, right?

When did you write your report in this case?

You also filled out some field notes, correct?

You filled those out while this incident was still fresh in your recollection?

And part of the reason that you did that was so that you can remember all the important details?

Because you're aware when you write a report that it could be months before you testify about the incident, correct?

In a DWI investigation, or an actual physical control investigation, you're especially careful to note all the signs of impairment that you observe, is that right?

This wasn't the only DWI arrest you made that month, was it?

It is important to write good reports so you don't confuse the facts of one case with another, right?

If you write sloppy or inaccurate reports, you could face criticism or even discipline from someone in your department, isn't that true?

There are several strong incentives for you to write accurate, complete reports in every case, true?

When you write your reports, then, you include all of the facts important to the case, right?

And your memory was better at the time that you wrote these reports, than it would be today, correct?

You're no different than the rest of us; by that I mean your memory of older events doesn't get better over time, does it?

So if there is a conflict between your report and your recollection of events today while you testify, your report is likely to be more accurate than your recollection, true?

If your report does not include a particular fact, we can assume that it didn't happen, can't we?

For example, if your report does not say my client stumbled on his way from his vehicle back to your squad car, we can assume that he did not stumble, can't we? (I would not be so quick to agree to this assertion. It may be that you were very busy at the time you wrote the report and, although you tried to be thorough, you did not necessarily include every detail in your report. If you wrote into your report every detail that a lawyer later thought was important, your reports would be book-length. An honest response might be, "I don't know if you can assume that, because it was crazy busy that night and I had other things I had to do. I try hard to write thorough reports but I'm human and sometimes I may omit a detail which I can remember later if asked about it. And sometimes I make a mistake when writing a report.")

An important fact, like a sign of impairment, you would ordinarily include in your report, right?

You might respond, "Ordinarily, yes, but as I explained before, I'm not perfect."

There are several things you look for that may indicate someone is under the influence of alcohol, am I correct?

For example, you look for slurred speech, balance problems, and the like, correct?

In fact, the National Highway and Traffic Safety Administration lists 24 separate indicators of impairment?

You were trained to look for these signs of impairment, weren't you?

The attorney may then ask a litany of questions about the absence of impairment indicators. Depending on which indicators are stated in your arrest report, the questions will be designed to show the client did not exhibit many or most of them. For example ...

Was my client cooperative with you?

He never swore at you? Yelled at you? Treated you with disrespect?

You look for belligerence among people you suspect of impaired driving, don't you?

That is because belligerence can be a sign of impairment, correct?

If, while you are on the witness stand, you remember an indicator of impairment which was not listed in your arrest report, defense counsel may take one of two approaches. Taking the first approach, counsel may attack you immediately and imply that you are fabricating testimony in order to gain a conviction. The questioning may go like this:

> You say my client leaned against his truck when he was walking back to your squad car?
>
> And you considered that a sign of impairment, didn't you?
>
> Was it one of the factors you relied upon in deciding whether to arrest my client? (Attorney asks the court for permission to approach the witness, which is granted. Attorney shows the officer a copy of the incident report.)
>
> Is this the report you wrote in this case?
>
> You testified earlier that your report was written shortly after the incident when your memory of the event was fresh?
>
> Look through your report, officer. Take your time. Show me where in your report you mentioned that my client leaned on his truck.
>
> It is not there, is it?
>
> Does your department give out awards to the officers who make the most DWI arrests in a year?

Alternatively, counsel may save the attack for summation. Following this course, the attorney will make a note of your statement, sometimes by writing it down on a legal pad with dramatic flourish. In closing argument, counsel will remind the jury of your testimony concerning complete and accurate reports. Counsel will then argue you were dishonest, incompetent, or both, and that you should not be believed.

Finally, an attorney may attack your memory for the events leading up to the arrest with questions like these:

> Would you describe the clothes my client wore that night?
>
> What kind of shoes was he wearing?
>
> Without looking at your report, how tall was he?
>
> How much did he weigh?
>
> Was the parking lot lighted?
>
> What were the weather conditions at the time of the stop?
>
> Was there traffic in the area while you were conducting the field sobriety tests?

> Did you issue any other citations during your shift that day?
>
> Who did you issue a citation to immediately before my client?
>
> Who did you issue a citation to immediately after my client?
>
> Is it possible that you may have mixed up the facts from one of those other cases with this one?
>
> When did you start your shift that day?

All of these tactics are ethical and several of them may be employed in the course of one cross-examination. Prepare for them, first by noting details and including them in your incident report, and secondly by thinking about how you will answer the questions in your particular case.

Glossary

This is not intended to be a comprehensive list of terms. The best legal dictionary is *Black's Law Dictionary*. There are several legal glossaries available on the Internet, including dictionary.law.com and www.nolo.com.

acquittal: a decision by the judge or jury that the defendant is not guilty.

action: another word for lawsuit. "This action was started by the filing of the summons and complaint."

admission: an out-of-court statement by your adversary that you offer into evidence as an exception to hearsay rule. It may also be a statement that certain facts are true made in response to a request from the other side during discovery.

affidavit: a written document in which a person swears under oath that something is true.

affirm: a decision by an appellate court upholding a ruling made by a trial court judge or jury; also the promise of a witness to tell the truth. Some witnesses prefer not to "swear to tell the truth" and are asked to "affirm under the penalty of perjury to tell the truth."

affirmative defense: an explanation for a defendant's actions that excuses or justifies otherwise criminal behavior. Some common affirmative defenses include self-defense, insanity, duress, and intoxication.

answer: a legal document outlining the response of a defendant to allegations made in the complaint; in the criminal law arena, the defendant does not file an answer because she or he is presumed innocent.

appeal: a written request to a higher court to modify or reverse the judgment of a lower court. Appellate courts generally accept as true all the facts that the trial judge or jury found to be true, and decide only whether a judge made mistakes in applying the law. If the appellate court decides that a mistake was made which affected the outcome, it will direct the lower court to conduct a new trial. Often, mistakes are deemed "harmless" and the judgment is left alone.

bail (also called "**bond**"): a sum of money filed with the court by a defendant to assure that she or he will return to court for future proceedings. Courts generally consider three factors in setting bond: the seriousness of the offense, the likelihood the defendant will flee, and the safety of the community.

bailiff: a person appointed by the judge to keep order in the courtroom and to keep others from contacting the jury while jurors deliberate.

bench trial: a trial where the judge, not a jury, decides the case.

burden of proof: the obligation of a party to prove something is true. In criminal cases the burden is on the prosecution to prove the defendant's guilt by proof "beyond a reasonable doubt." In civil cases, the plaintiff must prove entitlement to win by a "preponderance of the evidence," sometimes described as proving it is more likely than not true.

chambers: the judge's office.

civil: that part of the law that encompasses business, contracts, estates, domestic (family) relations, accidents, negligence and lawsuits, but is not criminal law.

civil action: any lawsuit relating to civil matters and not criminal prosecution.

complaint: a legal document which outlines the allegations made by the plaintiff against the defendant[s].

contempt of court: behavior in or out of court that violates a court order, or otherwise disrupts or shows disregard for the court. Refusing to answer a proper question, to file court papers on time, or to follow local court rules can expose witnesses, lawyers and litigants to contempt findings. Contempt of court is punishable by fine or imprisonment.

continuance: the postponement of a hearing, trial, or other scheduled court proceeding, at the request of one or both parties, or by the judge without consulting them.

criminal complaint: a document which contains the specific allegations of a criminal charge against a defendant, e.g., "On June 13, the defendant, Stick E. Fingers, committed Theft of Property when he took a carton of cigarettes from the 7-11 Store without paying for it."

cross-examination: questioning done by the party who did not call the witness to the stand. Cross-examination is characterized by the frequent use of leading questions.

damages: in a lawsuit, the amount of money a party received as a result of injury or loss caused by the other party.

defendant: the party against whom a case is brought in court. In the criminal arena, the defendant is the person charged with committing an offense. In a civil case, the defendant is the party who is being sued for damages.

deponent: the person who is questioned during a deposition.

deposition: testimony taken under oath before trial and recorded by a court reporter. Sometimes videotaped, excerpts from the transcript of a deposition can be used as evidence at trial.

direct examination: questioning done by the attorney who calls the witness to the stand.

discovery: the investigation done by the parties before trial. It may consist of interrogatories (a list of written questions), requests for admissions, or depositions. The object of discovery is to discover the strengths and weaknesses of the other side's case.

DWI: [Driving While Intoxicated] the crime of operating a motor vehicle while under the influence of alcohol or drugs, including prescription drugs. Complete intoxication is not required; the level of alcohol or drugs in the driver's body must simply be enough to prevent him from thinking clearly or driving safely. State laws specify the levels of blood alcohol content at which a person is presumed to be under the influence. Also called DUI or Driving While Under the Influence, or Driving Under the Influence.

elements of a crime: the parts or components of an offense which the prosecution must prove beyond a reasonable doubt. For example, the elements for a DWI charge are: 1. The defendant 2. drove or was in actual physical control of a motor vehicle 3. on a public way 4. while under the influence of alcohol or drugs 5. on a specific day 6. within the boundaries of the city, county, or district over which the court has jurisdiction.

evidence: information presented to a judge or jury designed to convince them of the truth or falsity of key facts. Evidence typically includes testimony of witnesses, documents, photographs, records, videos, and laboratory reports.

exclusionary rule: a court-created rule which disallows use of evidence at trial which was obtained illegally, e.g., the drugs found during a warrantless search of a house will not be admitted as evidence in a drug possession trial.

felony: a serious crime, usually punishable by more than one year imprisonment. It is contrasted with misdemeanors and infractions, less serious offenses. Examples of felonies include murder, rape, burglary, and aggravated assault.

finder-of-fact: the person or persons who will decide the case; the judge in a bench trial, or the jury in a jury trial.

fishing expedition: legal grasping at straws; the use of pre-trial investigation (discovery) or witness questioning in an unfocused attempt to uncover damaging evidence for use against an adversary.

hearsay: an out-of-court statement offered in court to prove the truth of the matter asserted in the statement, e.g., "John told me the light at the intersection was green when he entered it."

Hearsay Rule: a rule of evidence prohibiting consideration of secondhand testimony at a trial. For example, if an eyewitness to an accident later tells another person what she saw, the second person's testimony would normally be excluded from a trial by the hearsay rule. Secondhand testimony is thought to be inherently unreliable because the opposing party has no ability to confront and cross-examine the person who has firsthand knowledge of the event. However, there are many exceptions to the hearsay rule governing situations where courts have concluded that a particular type of hearsay is likely to be reliable. These exceptions include statements by the defendant, statements made by an opposing party which contradict what she said in court (called "admissions against interest"), government records, statements of dying people, spontaneous statements (something a person blurts out when excited or startled), and statements about a person's state of mind or future intentions, to name just a few.

HGN test: Horizontal Gaze Nystagmus test. One of three standardized field sobriety tests endorsed by the National Highway Traffic and Safety Administration. The presence of nystagmus or twitching of the eyeball is an indicator of impairment due to alcohol consumption.

hostile witness: a witness who is likely biased against the party represented by the questioner. During direct examination, a lawyer is usually not allowed to ask leading questions of their own witness. But if the witness shows open hostility to the interests (or the person) represented by a lawyer, that lawyer may ask the court to declare the witness "hostile." If the judge so declares, the lawyer may ask the witness leading questions.

hung jury: a jury which is unable to reach a verdict. When there is a hung jury, the judge will declare a mistrial. The case can then be tried again to another jury. More frequently, the case is settled by the parties if it is a lawsuit for damages, or resolved by a plea bargain if it involves a criminal charge.

impeach: to discredit a witness's testimony by showing the witness is not believable; also, the process of charging an official with misconduct warranting removal from office.

inadmissible evidence: testimony or other evidence that fails to meet court standards governing the types of evidence that can be presented to a judge or jury. When evidence is ruled inadmissible, it is usually because it falls into a category deemed so unreliable that a court should not consider it in deciding a case. For example, hearsay evidence, or an expert's opinion that is not based on facts generally accepted in the field, is inadmissible. Evidence may also be declared inadmissible if it will take too long to present or risks inflaming the jury, as might be the case with graphic pictures of a homicide victim. In criminal cases, evidence gathered illegally is commonly ruled inadmissible.

information: a legal document which sets forth the criminal charge against a defendant. In many jurisdictions, the information is used for felonies while a criminal complaint is used for misdemeanors and infractions.

infraction: a minor violation of the law, e.g., careless driving. Infractions are typically punishable only by fine; no jail time can be imposed.

interrogatories: written questions sent by one party to a lawsuit to an opposing party. They are designed to discover key facts about an opponent's case. Interrogatories must be answered under penalty of perjury. Court rules regulate how, when, and how many interrogatories can be asked.

judgment: a final ruling by the court resolving the key questions in a lawsuit and determining the rights and obligations of the opposing parties. In a criminal case, the judgment is synonymous with the final sentence imposed on the defendant.

jurisdiction: the authority of a court to hear and decide a case. To make a legally valid decision in a case, a court must have both "subject matter jurisdiction" (power to hear the type of case in question, which is granted by the state legislatures and Congress) and "personal jurisdiction" (power to make a decision affecting the parties involved in the lawsuit, which a court gets as a result of the parties' actions). The term jurisdiction is also commonly used to define the amount of money a court has the power to award. For example, small claims courts have jurisdiction only to hear cases up to a certain monetary amount, typically $10,000. If a court doesn't have personal jurisdiction over all the parties and the subject matter involved, it "lacks jurisdiction," which means it doesn't have the power to render a decision.

juror: one who sits on a jury. The names of potential jurors are typically generated from lists of motor vehicle drivers and voters. Jury service is a duty and failure to heed a jury summons is punishable by fine and imprisonment. Jurors receive little compensation for service.

jury: a group of people selected to apply the law, as stated by the judge, to the facts of a case and render a decision, called the verdict. Traditionally, an American jury was made up of twelve people who had to arrive at a unanimous decision. But today, in many states, juries in civil cases may be composed of as few as six members and non-unanimous verdicts may be permitted. Most states still require twelve-person, unanimous verdicts for criminal trials of felonies, though misdemeanors may be tried to a six-person jury. Some courts allow jurors to ask questions, in writing, especially in civil cases.

jury nullification: a decision by the jury to acquit a defendant who has violated a law that the jury believes is unjust or wrong. Jury nullification has always been an option for juries in England and the United States, although judges will prevent a defense lawyer from urging the jury to acquit on this basis. Nullification appears in criminal cases when the jury disagrees with the punishment—for example, in "three strikes" cases when the jury realizes that conviction of a relatively minor third offense will result in lifetime imprisonment.

leading question: a question which suggests the answer, e.g., "You were at home around 9:30 on the evening of May 3, weren't you?"

liable: legally responsible. For example, a person may be liable for a debt, liable for an accident due to careless behavior, liable for failing do something required by a contract, or liable for the commission of a crime. Someone who is found liable for an act or omission must usually pay damages or, if the act was a criminal one, face punishment.

malpractice: the delivery of substandard care or services by a lawyer, doctor, dentist, accountant, or other professional. Generally, malpractice occurs when a professional fails to provide the quality of care that should reasonably be expected in the circumstances, with the result that a patient or client is harmed.

misdemeanor: a criminal offense less serious than a felony. Misdemeanors are usually punishable by no more than one year in jail and a fine. Examples of misdemeanors include DWI, Simple Assault, and Possession of Drug Paraphernalia.

motion: during a lawsuit, a request to the judge for a decision—called an order or ruling—to resolve procedural or other issues that come up during litigation. For example, after receiving hundreds of irrelevant interrogatories, a party might file a motion asking that the other side be ordered to stop engaging in unduly burdensome discovery. A motion can be made before, during, or after trial. Typically, one party submits a written motion to the court, at which point the other party has the opportunity to file a written response. The court then often schedules a hearing at which each side delivers a short oral argument. The court then approves or denies the motion. Most motions cannot be appealed until the case is over.

nolo contendere (also called **"no contest"**): a plea entered by the defendant in response to being charged with a crime. The defendant who pleads nolo contendere neither admits nor denies committing the crime, but agrees there is enough evidence for the prosecution to convict. The defendant pleading nolo contendere is sentenced just as if she or he was found guilty. Usually, this type of plea is entered because it can't be used as an admission of guilt if a civil case is held after the criminal trial.

non-leading question: a question which does not suggest the answer, e.g., "Where were you on the evening of May 3rd?"

objection: a point of law raised by an attorney seeking a ruling by the judge.

one-leg stand test: One of three standardized field sobriety tests endorsed by the National Highway Traffic and Safety Administration. This divided-attention test is designed to check a subject's balance as well as the ability to follow instructions. It requires a subject to hold one leg aloft for several seconds without swaying, raising arms for balance, or putting the foot down.

overruled: a decision whereby the judge disagrees with the point of law raised by an attorney who made the objection.

pain and suffering: physical or emotional distress resulting from an injury for which a plaintiff can seek compensation in the form of money.

party: a person, corporation, or other legal entity that files a lawsuit (the "plaintiff" or "petitioner") or defends against one (the "defendant" or "respondent"). In a criminal case, the parties are "The State of (Florida)" or "The City of (Orlando)" and "(John Jones), the defendant." *See* "plaintiff" and "defendant."

PBT: Preliminary breath test. A test administered at the place of the stop using a portable breath device capable of determining the breath alcohol content of a driver. Many jurisdictions do not allow these test results to be used at trial but only for determining if an officer had probable cause to arrest.

plaintiff: the party who brings a case to court; in the criminal law arena, the plaintiff is the governmental body that brings the charges against the defendant.

plea bargain: a negotiation between the defendant and his attorney on one side and the prosecutor on the other, in which the defendant agrees to plead "guilty" or "no contest" to some crimes, in return for reduction of the severity of the charges, dismissal of some of the charges, the prosecutor's willingness to recommend a particular sentence, or some other benefit to the defendant. Sometimes the bargain requires the defendant to reveal information such as location of stolen goods, or the names of others participating in the crime. Reasons for the bargain include a desire to cut down on the number of trials, danger to the defendant of a long term in prison if convicted, and the ability to get information on criminal activity from the defendant.

pro se: a Latin phrase meaning "for himself" or "on one's own behalf." This term denotes a person who represents herself in court. Among trial veterans, the defendant in a criminal case acting pro se is derisively referred to as a self-basting turkey.

prosecutor: one employed by a governmental body to bring charges and litigate criminal cases.

public defender: one employed by a governmental body to represent and defend persons accused of crimes when they cannot afford to hire an attorney.

recess: a break in the trial.

remand: to send back, e.g., the appellate court reversed the conviction and remanded the case to the trial court with instructions to give the defendant a new trial.

rest: what an attorney says to a judge to signal that there are no additional witnesses or evidence to be presented by the party represented by that attorney, e.g., "The Plaintiff rests, Your Honor."

sequestration: an order of the judge requiring witnesses to stay out of the courtroom until they've testified; also the order of a judge requiring the jury to stay together until it has reached a verdict.

self-incrimination: making statements that might expose one to criminal prosecution, presently or in the future. The Fifth Amendment to the U.S. Constitution prohibits the government from forcing anyone to provide evidence (as in answering questions) that might lead to the person being prosecuted for a crime.

Statute of Limitations: the time limit within which a lawsuit or criminal charges must be filed. The exact limit varies with the kind of lawsuit, the seriousness of the charge, and the state or federal court in which the action is filed. If the lawsuit or criminal charges are filed too late, the case will be dismissed if the issue is raised.

subpoena (also spelled "**subpena**"): a court order issued at the request of a party requiring a witness to appear in court.

subpoena duces tecum: a type of subpoena, usually issued at the request of a party, by which a witness is ordered to produce certain documents at a deposition or trial.

summons: a document prepared by the plaintiff and issued by a court informing the defendant that she or he has been sued. The summons requires the defendant to file a response with the court within a given time period or risk losing the case under the terms of a default judgment.

suppress: to keep out, e.g., the judge determined the defendant's confession was not voluntary and suppressed it.

sustained: a decision whereby the judge agrees with the point of law raised by an attorney who made the objection.

testify: to provide oral evidence under oath at trial or at a deposition.

transcript: a document prepared by a court reporter setting forth the words and activities at a hearing, trial, or deposition.

verdict: the decision of the jury or judge.

voir dire: the process of questioning prospective jurors; literally "to speak the truth."

walk-and-turn test: one of three standardized field sobriety tests endorsed by the National Highway Traffic and Safety Administration. This divided-attention test is designed to check a subject's balance as well as the ability to follow instructions. It involves taking nine steps, heel-to-toe, pivoting, and returning nine steps to the starting point.

witness: one who provides testimony under oath at a trial or deposition.

Notes

1. Craig Townsend, *Mind Training Tips for Swimmers*, http://swimming.about.com/od/swimmingmindtrainingtips/qt/visualize_succe.htm

2. Jennifer Lawler & David Lignell, *eHow to Become Proficient in the Martial Arts Through Visualization*, www.ehow.com.

3. James Rasicot, *New Techniques for Winning Jury Trials*. (Minneapolis: AP Publications, 1990).

4. John T. Molloy, *Dress For Success*. (New York: Peter H. Wyden, 1975).

5. Oliver W. Sacks, *The Man Who Mistook His Wife for a Hat: And Other Clinical Tales* (New York: Harper Perennial, 1990).

6. Kenji Kitao and S. Kathleen Kitao, *Intercultural Nonverbal Communication: A Bibliography*, http://eric.ed.gov/?id=ED285402.

7. Timothy P. Maher, *The Information Needs of Jurors in Complex Litigation*, www.wolftechnical.com/webfocus/infoneedsjur.pdf.

8. Loftus, E. F. & Zanni, G. (1975). *Eyewitness testimony: The influence of the wording of a question*. Bulletin of Psychonomic Society, 5, 19–31.

9. Francis L. Wellman, *The Art of Cross-Examination*. (New York: Dorset Press, 1986).

10. Edward W. Cleary, *McCormick's Handbook of the Law of Evidence*. (St. Paul: West Publishing Co., 1972).

11. Loftus, E.F. (1979). *Eyewitness testimony*. Cambridge, MA: Harvard University Press.

12. Barron, B., Henderson, M. & Spurgeon, R. 1994. Effects of time of day instruction on reading achievement of below grade readers. Reading Improvement, 31(1), 56–60.

13. Intons Peterson, M.J., Rocchi, P., West, T., McLellan, K. and Hackney, A. 1999. Age, testing at preferred or non-preferred times (testing optimality), and false memory. Journal of Experimental Psychology: Learning, Memory, and Cognition, 25(1), 2340.

14. Ryan, L., Hatfield, C. & Hofstetter, M. 2002. Caffeine Reduces Time-of-Day Effects on Memory Performance in Older Adults. Psychological Science, 13 (1), 6871.

15. Speidel, G. E., & Troy, M. E. (1985). Imagery in the educational process. In A. A. Sheikh & K. S. Sheikh (Eds.), Imagery in education, imagery in the educational process. New York: Baywood Publishing.

16. Paivio, A. (1969). Mental imagery in associative learning and memory. Psychological Review, 76, 241–263.

17. Burns, Marcelline, Ph.D., Horizontal Gaze Nystagmus: The Science and the Law: A Resource Guide for Judges, Prosecutors and Law Enforcement, American Prosecutors Research Institute, National Traffic Law Center (1999).

18. The Arizona Supreme Court's decision in *State v. Superior Court* is the seminal case on admissibility of HGN test results. In that case, the lower court received voluminous testimony on the scientific basis and reliability of the test. The Arizona Supreme Court also consulted numerous treatises, articles, and empirical studies discussing the scientific basis for the test, and compiled a lengthy bibliography of those sources. See *State v. Superior Court*, 718 P.2d at 182–184. Based upon the expert testimony and written authorities, the court concluded that the HGN test had gained general acceptance in the scientific community, and that it therefore satisfied the requirements of *Frye v. United States*, 293 F. 1013 (D.C.Cir. 1923).

19. *City of McLaughlin v. Fargo*, 515 N.W. 2D 700 (N.D. 1994). An officer will not be permitted to testify, for example, that detection of four out of six clues means there is a 70% chance the subject had an alcohol concentration level of .08 or greater at the time of testing.

20. *State v. Homan*, 732 N.E.2d 952 (Ohio 2000). The court applied this same standard to the walk-and-turn and one-leg stand test.

Index